ABOVE

Sydney

PHOTOGRAPHY BY

GEORGE HALL

TEXT BY

NICHOLAS BRASH

DESIGNED BY ADRIAN YOUNG

WATTLE
BOOKS

The New South Wales golf course ... runs
right to the Pacific Ocean.

Managing Editor: Mary-Dawn Earley
Editor: Nicholas Brash
Cecille Weldon: Production Manager
Additional photography: Leo Meier

Preceding pages:

Page 1
The Pacific crashes on to the sandstone cliffs
of South Head.

Pages 2-3
Rock fishing: a great Sydney tradition.

Pages 4-5
Surfing ... as natural in Sydney as the waves
rolling in.

Pages 6-7
If you can't make the beach ... a back yard
pool will cool you down.

Published by Kevin Weldon and Associates Pty
Ltd, 43 Victoria Street, McMahons Point,
NSW 2060, Australia.
First published 1984.
©Copyright Kevin Weldon 1984.
Typeset in Australia by Smith & Miles
Printed by Dai Nippon Printing Co. Ltd. Tokyo.

National Library of Australia Cataloguing-in-
Publication Data
Hall, George (George N.).
  Above Sydney
  ISBN 0 949708 08 9.
  1. Sydney (N.S.W.) — Aerial Photographs.
  I. Title.
919.44'1

Designed by Adrian Young

**A Kevin Weldon Production
in association with Channel 7, Sydney.**

Contents

The Archibald Fountain . . . designed by
French sculptor Francois Sicard in 1932 as a
monument to those who served in World War I.

Acknowledgements

The Pilots

Grant Johnson, Danny Tyler, Nick Ross, Vic Walton, Aquatic Airways, Noel Dodwell, Tim Joyce, Ross McDonald, David Voihth, Kevin Weldon, Dick Smith, Davey Jones, Bob Wightman, Lindsay Fitzgerald, Rob Haylock, Lionel 'Sam' Houston and a special acknowledgement to Channel Seven's chief pilot Frank van Rees

Also, thanks to
Kevin Hadley and Martin Hayley, *Dept of Main Roads*
Sonia Smirnow, *Regent Hotel*
Brian Baxter, *Centrepoint*
Jan Kaye, *Northpoint*
Chief Inspector Ray Sheppard and his crew of the *NSW Police Air Wing*
Colin Laurendet and Kerri Murphy, *Maritime Services Board*
Peter McCormick and the *Westpac Surf Rescue team*
Nola Furner
J. G. 'Ginty' Lush

Technical notes

With the exception of the historical shots and the 9″ by 9″ vertical mapping aerials, the entire book was photographed on Kodachrome transparency film with Nikon 35mm cameras and a variety of Nikkor lenses ranging from 15mm wide-angle to 300mm telephoto. For most of the helicopter work a Kenyon gyro-stabiliser was attached to the camera to counteract vibration.

Channel Seven's Bernie Keenan sways out of a network helicopter to catch his own view from above Sydney.

There is, according to George Hall, no better way to see the splendour of Sydney than from a helicopter … unless it's a Tiger Moth … or a seaplane. Hall, who spent three years zig-zagging Europe in the Goodyear blimps, used a variety of aircraft for his Sydney shoot. The police helicopters, Channel Seven's craft, the Westpac surf rescue helicopter and businessman Dick Smith's machine all gave him one perspective. Two seaplanes: Kevin Weldon's Cessna 182 and Vic Walton's Aquatic Airways Beaver gave him a new angle on the coastline and waterways. And to complement the aerial coverage, Hall was able to shoot from the highest points in Sydney … the Harbour Bridge, Northpoint, Centrepoint, and the Regent Hotel.

His fellow photographer, Leo Meier, shot New Year's Eve in Sydney from another vantage point: the AMP Building on the corner of Phillip and Young Streets. The City-to-Surf was photographed from Vic Walton's seaplane and the magnificent Sydney-Hobart yacht race from a Waterwings' Cessna 172. Together – and with the help of a lot of enthusiastic pilots – they have produced a unique and spectacular view of Australia's most spectacular city.

Shadows creep over Hyde Park but the park still offers a warm resting place in the heart of the city.

INTRODUCTION

THE SPRAY shoots off the green waves at Bondi, swept over the concrete retaining wall by the nor-easter to fall on the carpark where the tar has turned to black gum. *Summer in Sydney.* A sudden squall shoots up from the south, the temperature drops. Thunder gives a quick warning and unless you've listened and ducked for cover the southerly buster dumps its rain, laughs quickly and vanishes. *Spring squalls in Sydney.* The traffic chokes the Wakehurst Parkway: cars beating their way back from the Peninsula. A brand-new Rolls-Royce and a Porsche convertible crawl frustrated behind a multi-coloured Holden panel van. Bits of the original white shining through the pink primer. The newest thing is the roof rack carrying three surfboards. Across the rise and the frustration fades. The city unfolds … the lights fighting with the sunset to be seen. *Summer evenings in Sydney.* An old yawl strains through the Heads. Alongside her a Port Jackson shark glides near the surface, his light brown back catching the early sun. Not a powerboat in sight; only sailors make an early start. *Autumn sunrises in Sydney.* Office girls giggle out of their cages on the Quay, crossing to the flattened grass near the passenger dock. Behind them the historic Rocks stand as they've stood for nearly two centuries impassively watching the changes. Plastic bottles of orange juice and chicken sandwiches. *Winter lunches in Sydney.* Dame Joan Sutherland stands on the makeshift stage. The unemployed in jeans stand next to dresses that cost a year's dole. The Domain rings with Traviata; lit by the far-off glow of the arc lights at the SCG. The West Indies are playing Australia. *Summer nights in Sydney.* Sydney is feelings. There are statistics … the number of residents, the square area, the span of the Harbour Bridge, the number of rooms in the Opera House. You live here; you don't care about facts and figures. To live in Sydney is to feel alive, optimistic, peaceful. And one feeling above all: that glorious sensation that comes when your jumbo jet floats in. The Bridge is obvious, the Harbour shines, that orange building in North Sydney stands out. The red roofs smile up as the plane drops lower. You're Above Sydney and almost home.

THE WAVE

THE LAST ripple flopped exhausted on a mudbank in Carroll's Creek. A boy, wandering barefoot and feeling the mud squeal between his toes, kicked idly at a leaf in the puddle the ripple left ... all that remained of a wave that had weighed 30 tonnes as it raced over the Pacific, standing three metres tall in the troughs off the New South Wales coastline. It had cut itself at Barrenjoey, a little corner trickling

A handful of cars ... a sombre sky ... steely waters. Winter at Palm Beach. But, even in the grip of a grey day, Barrenjoey Head still looks majestic, the lighthouse looking down on Broken Bay and back to a deserted beach and a silent Pittwater where a handful of windsurfers risk being dumped in the chilly water.

into Broken Bay, the balance flowing down the coast. Into Palm Beach, around Little Head into Whale Beach and through Avalon, Bilgola and Newport. Still strong as it raced down the coastline, parts of it peeling off into the ocean beaches.

The beaches of Sydney. They seduce the Pacific and exhaust it. The open beaches such as South Curl Curl, still rated one of the most dangerous on the Sydney shore. The sheltered beaches and bays such as Harbord, where toddlers happily sit in the white ripples, stuffing sand and salt water in their mouths. Just around the corner from Curl Curl.

Narrabeen Lagoon narrows to a bottleneck and trickles round the horn of the beach to meet the sea. On the beach, swimmers and sunbathers carefully pick their way round the pegged-out replanting zones where plants will anchor the sand to prevent erosion. **Below:** A busier Palm Beach and Pittwater ... warmer weather has brought out the swimmers and the sailboard riders.

Over: A windsurfing class in the safety of Narrabeen Lagoon. They may look hopeless but they're being coached in the art of pulling up the sail after an inevitable tumble.

And Bondi. Before there was an Opera House, Sydney was famous for Bondi Beach. The rest of the world knows only the postcard Bondi, the stretch of golden sand and the blue sky. Sydney knows another Bondi, the smell of the beach and the bay … something no postcard can carry. The smell of green waves and their salty spray. The smell of litres of suntan lotion and zinc; the fish and chips lying just two towel lengths away, their owner flat on her back, topless and eyes closed, sticking out a roaming hand for the bag. The seagulls above, trying to pluck up the courage to land on their blood-webbed feet and steal a chip, just one.

The smell of an old panel van with worn-out rings, its black smoke drifting from the exhaust down the stone and concrete wall on to the beach. This is Bondi. Where Lebanese of different sects sit side by side, far from the strife of Beirut; where Serbs and Croats walk the same path

of sand or Turks and Armenians stand in the same queue at the 30 Flavours ice-cream shop. The beach is the great Australian leveller. The sun and the surf are enough. It's too hard to squabble on a Sydney beach.

Bondi is seedy now, a vast plain of red roofs and like any desert, short on trees. Greed has seen a shanty town spring up where there could well have been a St Tropez. But it has kept Bondi within reach of everyone. Sydneysiders and tourists are disappointed at the decline of Bondi the suburb. But, by not 'going exclusive', everyone can afford to share it. The Bondi ghetto can always be cleaned up; it is beginning now with

Left: The Corso stretches down to South Steyne at Manly, a placid pedestrian mall where summer visitors pick at pizza, pies and pineapple ice-cream in the rash of takeaway shops. **Above:** Treacherous Curl Curl. That golden stretch of sand looks innocent but a savage rip runs along the beach with an undertow than can sweep a weak swimmer under and out. **Over:** They line the beach like children at a Little Athletics meeting, confused and eager. The 1984 Board Sailing Marathon, from Manly Pier to the Spit Bridge and back, was a gruelling 15 km.

new foreshore apartment blocks. And the beach will never deteriorate.

At the southern end of the beach a group of Indestructibles meets each morning. Each morning ... including the middle of winter when a southerly wind cuts into the bay. The water temperature plummets as the melting ice flows to the south chill the polar current sweeping up the east coast. These men, the Bondi Icebergs, have carried on a tradition of swimming all year round that began in 1929. (The same year the last shark attack was recorded at Bondi Beach.)

From the Icebergs' corner a path winds up the headland; taking in the superb view of the Pacific flowing down to the southern beaches. The track winds round to Tamarama, a superb view. A small bay of white sand framed by a green shelf. And on the beach, crowded side by side, lie topless sunbathers, motionless — a sea of brown and bronze bodies. Occasionally someone raises the energy to flop into the sea.

Some naked, some near naked. The rocks at Reef Beach soak up the heat for the dedicated sunbaker. Reef Beach is one of Sydney's two official nudist beaches.

Left: It seems like taking coals to Newcastle: building a water fun park at Manly. But the Waterworks is a favourite with families. **Mid-Left:** And so is the gentle water of Shelley Beach, a short walk from the Manly beachfront. **Bottom Left:** As the sun sets, it highlights the magnificent 'Cardinal's Palace'...

Below: The Manly Ferry pulls away from the pier on the city run. From above, looking over Manly to the north, the beaches and the bays stretch up to the tip of the Peninsula.

Around the southern horn of Kurnell Peninsula, where Captain Cook landed, is Sydney's longest ocean beach, Wanda. Here, 4km of white sand stretches in an arc, blurring into Cronulla beach at its southermost point. The southern beaches tend to be overlooked by Sydney. But the lifesavers of Wanda and Cronulla have always been among the country's best. They've needed to be.

Manly and the beaches up the coast are much better known. Manly is a seaside village, actually making the map before Sydney. Captain Phillip left the swamps of Botany Bay to head for the fine harbour Cook had recorded in his journal ... the harbour of Port Jackson. Phillip turned

hard right inside the Heads, ending up in Manly inlet, before heading up Harbour to what is now The Rocks. The Norfolk Island pines which line the Manly foreshore are gradually dying, crushed by salt spray and pollution. But if Bondi is known for its postcard image of golden beaches and brown bodies, Manly is recognised by its pines.

On the ocean side of Manly, but tucked in safely behind the southern headland is Fairy Bower and Shelly Beach, a gentle flat stroll from the Ferry Wharf ... that's if you've survived the crowd cramming into the Manly Fun Pier and Shark Aquarium. Shelly Beach is just that ... shelly. But it's very fine shell, woven into the sand, comfortable to lie on and a beach nearly always free from wind.

The two white knights of Sydney...the Macquarie Lighthouse pointing to the Opera House.

Today, Manly like every beach in Sydney is packed in summer. It is strange to realise that a city which lives for its beaches could introduce an Act in 1838 which effectively prohibited all swimming except between 8pm and 6am.

In 1902 the local newspaper editor William Gocher decided enough was enough. He surfed in broad daylight and then sat on the beach. When he wasn't arrested thousands of overheated, frustrated swimmers began to follow his lead. Sydney took to the beaches at it was meant to. William Gocher was a pioneer. So too were Frank McElhone and the Reverend McKeown at Bondi. Like Gocher they frolicked in the surf at midday and, similarly, were not arrested though the police were on the beach watching. But if the three beaching musketeers won that round they still had to contend with the neck-to-knee costumes. In 1907 that

At the southern end of Bondi Beach, the home of the Bondi Icebergs, that band of hardy men who swim every day of the year. Behind the saltwater pool, Pacific Palisades, a luxury complex of apartments and penthouses that could mark the start of a new Bondi.

Over: A familiar sight at Australian surf carnivals, lifesavers and their surfboats.

The Opera House as Sydney has seen it every
New Year's Eve for the past eight years ... lit
up by a giant fireworks display which covers
the city with a 15-minute glitter.

Downtown Sydney lit with that special glow . . .

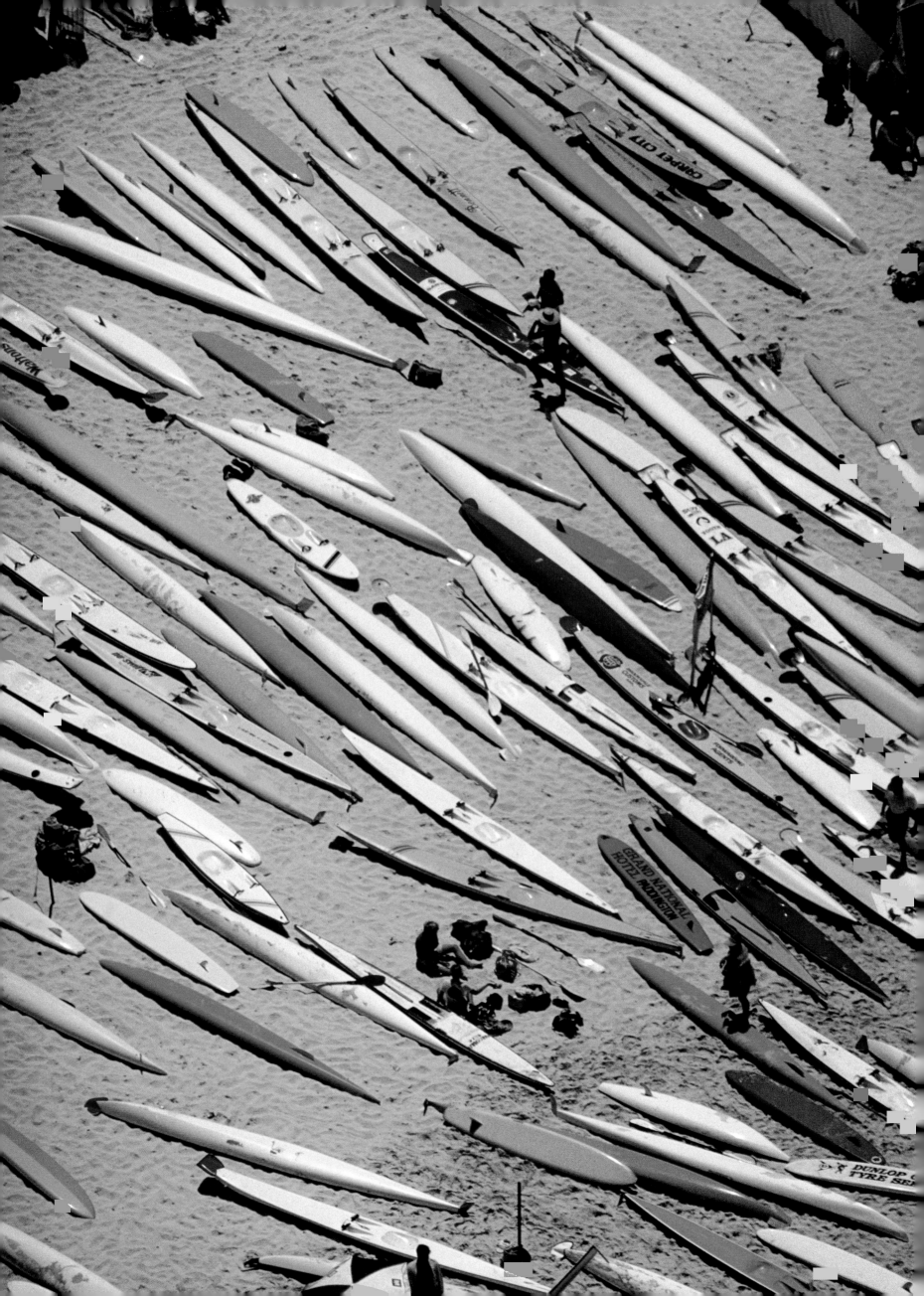

Bondi ... scene of a million postcards. And on the preceding page competitors' surf skis at the State Bank sponsored Surf Lifesaving Carnival.

finally came adrift ... literally. Swimmers, men and women, wore skirts to highlight the absurdity of the costume and took them off on the beach. Then came the brief one piece, finally the bikini and ultimately the topless 'suit'. Each reduction has been matched by a public outcry. But there was more to come. Or less ... the State Government set aside a number of beaches for nude sunbathing. One is Lady Bay, the outermost beach on south head; another is Reef Beach near Manly. For the past eight years Sydney has survived the nude beaches ... a far cry from the days when it was forbidden to swim in daylight, regardless of what you wore.

It's one of the world's great views, but you'd never know it. These houses at North Bondi turn their back on the Pacific Ocean and face their little street. **Above:** Lurline Bay, Coogee, where one of Sydney's many Edgecliff avenues runs down to form a T-junction with Seaside Avenue.
Right: Somehow the brownest bodies are at Tamarama, Bondi's southern neighbour. Pale newcomers work their way up to Tamarama.
Over: It's not enough to have the ocean spread out before you ... at Lurline Bay, the pools run to the cliff edge.

Hired umbrellas dot Lady Robinson's Beach at Botany Bay . . . where wary sunbathers find comfort together. **Below:** Marine Parade, Maroubra . . . houses, flats and pubs living happily on the edge of the reserve and the ocean. At the water's edge, Mahon Pool offers safe swimming among the rocks.

Lazy Brighton-le-Sands where a handful of sunbathers watch the mini-catamarans fooling about on the water's edge.
Below: Maroubra Beach Hotel in Marine Parade ... a beer garden oasis of umbrellas down by the sea. **Over:** Cronulla, with the beach in the background, runs down to Hungry Point with the Glaister Point baths jutting into the ocean and its own little pocket beach.

North of Manly, past the sheltered retreat of Harbord is the exposed bay of Curl Curl Beach. Not for the faint-hearted or indifferent swimmer. Here the ocean seems determined to batter the coast in at least one spot. The northern point of Dee Why Head gives little shelter; wild unruly waves crash in. No gentle rolling pattern here; they criss-cross each other, sweeping in at odd angles and pounding the sand. A savage undertow tears at the legs of swimmers. The beach is windy and behind it tussocks and sand dunes stand between the beach and the coast road.

Inland from Curl Curl are the suburbs of Brookvale and Dee Why, sadly forced into light industry. The beaches run on, through Collaroy and Narrabeen, Warriewood and Mona Vale, Bungan and Newport. Finally to Whale Beach and Palm Beach where the beach towels are liable to have a French designer's imprint and the Eskies give way to elegant chillers. No cask white wine here ... Pol Roget or, if the locals are slumming it, imported beer. Ideally a Czechoslavakian or Dutch lager. The drinks change but the life is the same ... soaking up the sun and flouncing into the surf when it gets too hot. (A Rolls-Royce parked on the beachfront is no insurance against sunburn.)

The beaches. They're a drawcard for all Sydney. From the outer west they come on trains and buses. Inner city suburbs such as Balmain have their young surfers; they line up at bus stops in the early morning, catching the 433 to Central and another train or a bus from there. The car-happy surfers cruise the coast looking for elusive waves, listening to radio reports, ringing friends up and down the coast. Somewhere the right wave is breaking. It may only be for an hour or two. Surfers have to be mobile. Travelling light. A panel van, a board, a roof rack and a jar of zinc cream. You're in business.

Opposite: A lone powerboat ruffles the morning quiet of the Ku-Ring-Gai Chase waterways...his wake rocking the dead-still waters, his engine waking the lorikeets. And a houseboat sitting gently in the stream is about to be shocked awake. **Above:** At the opposite end of Sydney, Bundeena at the northern tip of the Royal National Park is waking up. **Left:** The inlets of Ku-Ring-Gai are a perfect retreat...often only boats have total access.

Places where you would love to live

Sydney is the daydream capital of the world. No-one on a Sunday drive or a walk in any one of a dozen spots can have failed to see somewhere they'd love to live, if only . . .

Pockets have been developed crassly and clumsily . . . such as the Blues Point Tower, that concrete splodge that mars Blues Point . . . but by far the bulk of the foreshores have been settled and developed with a certain grace. And much of the prime land in the city is natural parkland or Crown land.

The Naval Academy at Outer South Head What a glorious place for a home . . . the Pacific roaring and pounding on one side; the Harbour stretching to the little red light on the arch of the Harbour Bridge the other. And in front, Middle Harbour, stretching to join natural parkland reserves, and the Manly foreshore. From a sunshaded balcony, the best view of the Sydney-Hobart yacht race imaginable, picking up the sweat on the crew as they strain to be first through the Heads.

The quarantine station at __Quarantine Head__ Curled in behind the point of North Head, Quarantine Bay is a sheltered anchorage for weekend sailors.

The Waverley Cemetery at Clovelly Surely no other city in the world has such an idyllic resting place. The vast Waverley Cemetery spreads out to face the ocean, tumbling down to the edge of the coast.

The Bondi Public Golf Course The Japanese can't believe it ... they queue for hours to pay a fortune to play a game of golf in their own country. Here, for a couple of dollars they can stroll on to a magnificent nine-hole public golf course, the bunkers being natural pits in the sandy course. Two of the holes teeter nervously on the cliff edge. Bondi lies below and stretching away to the point where sea and sky blur together, the Pacific.

Garden Island It may be a hotpotch of scaffolding and cranes now. But imagine it as it was ... a humpbacked island separated from Potts Point by a narrow channel, close enough to build your own causeway but far enough to keep out the day trippers. A semi-island in the heart of the city. A clear view of the Opera House and looking up the Harbour to the Heads.

Bradleys Head With the Zoo for a neighbour, Bradleys Head shares a spectacular view of the main harbour and the eastern suburbs out through the Heads.

The Sacred Heart Convent at Rose Bay New South Head Road sweeps out of Rose Bay and rises up to Vaucluse. Midway up that rise, perched on the edge of the point, Sacred Heart Convent looks directly up the Harbour. It may not have that big Sydney selling point in real estate, a north-easterly aspect, but it does have a magnificent view. In the evening, as the sun sets shining through the spans of the Harbour Bridge, the city glows with a pink blush as the lights begin to take over from the day.

The Cardinal's Palace That magnificent building; at night standing out on the foothill rising above Manly to become the North Head lookout. Technically it's St Patrick's College, a Catholic seminary. But with that traditional European tower and Gothic magnificence the nickname has stuck.

THE WONDERFUL

A MIDDLE-AGED woman from San Francisco stood on the halfway mark on the steps climbing from The Rocks to the Harbour Bridge walkway. 'Gaad,' she said (or maybe it was 'Gawwd'), 'it's wonderful'. No-one had prepared her for the city of Sydney. They come from Paris, from Melbourne to scoff, from New York and New Zealand. The tourists. But nothing they've read, nothing they've been told has lived up

In the early morning the city is still drowsy. A ferry sets off for Manly to pick up the first commuters. No early morning sightseers have arrived at the Opera House...the liner *Canberra* has the city to herself as she is manoeuvred around the Opera House towards the passenger terminal at Circular Quay. **Over:** The late afternoon light on the Opera House casts an eerie reflection on the silver water.

to seeing the city for the first time. And that walk across the Harbour Bridge is a million-dollar view for free. The Opera House with its sails ...more has been written about them than the America's Cup. The spread of the city, the blocks of flats at Kirribilli with the ocean for a basement. The view up Parramatta River and the docks that should be ugly and depressing but have a charm of their own. In the middle of the day with the sun overhead bouncing down on the yachts skipping between the ferries; or in those quick moments before sunset when the city blushes. Sydney is addictive.

At Circular Quay a tiny ferry borrowed for the day from a commercial

Top: Even the cargo ships tied up at Darling Harbour look romantic in the fading summer light. **Above:** The Glebe Island Container Terminal, functional and orderly.
Opposite: They come from all round the world to sail on Sydney Harbour and for the Sydney to Hobart bluewater classic … the US yacht *Nirvana* flies her spinnaker proudly.
Bottom Right: The controversial aircraft carrier *Melbourne* at her final resting place, Garden Island.

Above: The Rocks ... narrow little streets where vintage pubs, warehouses and terrace houses squeeze together where The Rocks blur into Millers Point. **Right:** From the top of the Agar Steps a path leads to the Observatory, built in 1858. Parts of the wall surrounding the Observatory belong to the remains of Fort Phillip, built in 1804.

Opposite: The Rocks, nestling on the western side of the Harbour Bridge. From an historic start as Sydney's first development, The Rocks became fashionable and then slumped into decay from 1900 when the plague swept through the crowded area, forcing wholesale demolitions. The construction of the Bridge in the late 20s through to the early 30s saw more of The Rocks decay. Now it is being revived.

Left: The *Sun* City-to-Surf Fun Run goes under the Eastern Suburbs rail link. An institution, this 13th running drew 33 000 entrants. The most famous winner is marathon champion Robert de Castella who scored in 1981. **Below:** The city Bowling Club, opposite Hyde Park...a suburban institution in the heart of the city.

Mrs Macquarie's Chair, still one of Sydney's most peaceful spots for a picnic or to unwind at lunchtime, even at weekends when it is packed. And amazingly for the harbour of a major city, the water is clean and clear. The paths from the point wind back to the city, round to the Botanic Gardens or lazily along the water's edge to the Opera House.

shopping marina while the regular ferry has an overhaul slides past the *Oriana* berthed at the passenger dock. A hydrofoil skids round the Opera House and hoots impatiently...a ferry has overstayed at Quay No. 6. Tourists are pacing along the Quay, making the well-worn lap of The Rocks to the Opera House. And the city is shining. Overnight summer rain has washed down the skyscrapers, the rich patches of green under the bridge pylons and the Royal Botanic Gardens are vivid, the water takes its colour from the cloudless sky, shining blue and highlighting a small yacht skipping nervously past the ferries moving slowly out of the Quay.

The opening of the Opera House drew attention to one of Sydney's most beautiful walks — that stroll from Circular Quay around to Mrs Macquarie's Chair and up to the Botanic Gardens. The city is well-served with parks and green land. Centennial Park, opened officially in 1888 to mark the city's centenary played an even more important role in 1901...it was the scene of the Federation celebrations conducted by Australia's first Governor-General, Lord Hopetoun. And it must be one of the world's most magnificent city parks, bolstered by its neighbouring facilities, the Sydney Cricket Ground, Randwick Racecourse, Moore Park. But it was a close thing: the vast area, originally swampland, was

sold off in bits until Charles Moore, three times Mayor of Sydney, discovered the grant entitling the people of Sydney to the 200 hectare Common. At this time, too, the zoo was on the Moore Park side of the Common, which helped his cause.

He won. And today Centennial Park is one of the delights of Sydney. Joggers trip over the dogs — mongrels and exotic breeds — running across the grass; weekend cricketers use beer cans for boundary markers; Italian families have four-generation picnics. The park is a never-ending carousel. Originally, after the swampland had been reclaimed, it was laid out in the grand European manner; with sculptured lakes and horse-riding tracks. They still exist but Australian native flora have been introduced to give it a more natural feel.

Sadly, for visitors and tourists, the ferries no longer run along the eastern suburbs shoreline of the city. The lavish cruise ships point out

Government House...a semi-mediaeval design prepared in London in the 1830s by the royal architect, Edward Blore. Part of the Gothic revival that intoxicated Sydney at the time, it is one of the few gracious reminders of the mansions that used to look down on the Harbour from most points.

the places of interest but somehow they lack the fun of the creakers. The municipality of Woollahra runs from where the Cross sprawls drunkenly into Rushcutters Bay, to Watsons Bay. It takes in the diplomatic belt where discreet police watch over the consulates, spills into Australia's most expensive shopping village, Double Bay, doffs its cap at the wealth of Point Piper and runs through Vaucluse with its magnificent historic buildings and even more magnificent views.

Woollahra finishes at The Gap, a finishing point itself for many suicide victims, and the small bays of South Head. At Watson's Bay, Doyle's Restaurant has been serving meals on the beachfront for almost

Stately Sydney University... Australia's first university, designed in 1857. The quadrangle of neo-Gothic collegiate architecture and the old building with its great hall are reminders of the English university tradition.

Over: The lights are on at the Sydney Cricket Ground and for the next four hours the West Indies and Australia will fight out the second half of a day/night cricket clash.

100 years. There's scarcely a tourist with friends in Sydney who has been allowed to go home without the whiting or John Dory at Doyle's and too much Australian white wine. The Japanese tourists go a little farther along the shoreline. With undisguised glee groups of two or three men, immaculate in three-piece suits, stand in the summer heat on the cliff edge, their motorised Nikons at boiling point as they scan the nude bathers at Lady Bay.

Two of the area's more interesting historic buildings are the Rose Bay Police Station and Vaucluse House, vastly different but both picturesque. Vaucluse House is now a museum open to the public after beginning life as a stone cottage built by Irish convict turned wealthy landowner, Sir Henry Brown Hayes. Rose Bay Police Station was always a stone cottage, built in 1871 as a lodge for the Point Piper mansion Woollahra House, demolished in 1929.

Point Piper is Australia's millionaires' row, no matter what the people on the Swan River in Perth may feel. It boasts Australia's most expensive home, the summer residence of Robert Sangster and his wife Susan. They paid $6 million for it, buying it from photos provided by an architect friend. Tommy Smith, parks his Rolls-Royce nearby ... winning racehorses have been good to him. Entrepreneur turned film producer Michael Edgley built a home on the point. Less obvious millionaires enjoy the view more quietly as their stock portfolios compound.

Ironically, Point Piper is named after Captain John Piper who died

virtually penniless. He became one of the richest men in Sydney as the official collector of customs and harbour dues ... a top-of-the-harbour scheme. He entertained so lavishly at his Point Piper mansion that he was dubbed the crown prince of Australia. Governor Darling cut that short. When he landed in 1825 he very soon sacked Piper for neglect of duty. The luckless captain soon ran into financial difficulty and tried to commit suicide by jumping out of his boat. He was rescued by his staff and died 26 years later at the age of 78, the money spent and the memories dwindling.

But the city and the east is more than millionaires' mansions, skyscrapers and the sights of the Harbour Bridge and the Opera House. There's the versatile suburb of Paddington, where former workmen's terrace houses have become status living ... lacework and sandstone renovation is a booming business. Art galleries and comprehensive

A wet-suited windsurfer off Manly and heading for Spit Bridge in the 1984 Sail Board marathon. **Right:** The great bike race gets under way at intervals outside Parliament House in Macquarie Street.

Opposite (Top Left): The tables are set at Sydney's most magnificent dining room, the raised lawn at Kirribilli House. The garden setting of the Prime Minister's Sydney 'hotel' is Sydney's finest reminder of the 19th century style.

Opposite (Below): From the other side of the harbour the high-rise blocks and waterfront homes stare back at Kirribilli House.

Opposite (Top Right): On the Rose Bay side of Point Piper, mansions spill down to the water's edge, pools kissing the harbour water.

Above: The gentle green of Mrs Macquarie's Chair with the 'Boy' Charlton pool in the foreground and the curving path leading away to the Opera House above.

Opposite: It's early and the only queues at Doyle's famous fish restaurant are the dinghies. The Watsons Bay Hotel has its tables set in the beer garden and opening time is less than an hour away. Soon the queues will begin on the footpath to Doyle's next door. **Above:** Shark Bay, Vaucluse...where the iron net makes the name an empty threat and the swimmers are well protected. **Top:** Exclusive Wentworth Road curves around to become Fitzwilliam Road, opening up one of Sydney's smallest beaches, the white patch of Parsley Bay with its green reserve.

delicatessens mingle with the houses; unfortunately the dog droppings on the footpaths mingle with everyone. Sydney's growing gay community has Paddington as its base. Their tastes may not be everyone's preference but a network of excellent restaurants and antique shops has grown up around them.

At Rose Bay between the shopping wealth of Double Bay and the harbour views of Vaucluse, the seaplanes still set off on coastal sightseeing tours and commuter runs to Palm Beach. In the days when flying boats were an important form of air travel Rose Bay was Australia's main overseas air terminal. Today it is the setdown point for Aquatic Airways. Often for golfers in town for a day at Royal Sydney Golf Club.

Double Bay is Gucci territory. Gucci, St Laurent, Givenchy. If there's an expensive label it's on show in Double Bay. But it's also the main home of the NSW 18-ft Sailing League. Every Sunday from September to April the club holds challenge races. The sponsored yachts, their sails gleaming with hardware stores, TV stations and paint brands, fly across the water. *Presto,* an American yacht imported in 1854 began the craze that is still growing. Chartered ferries and launches follow the fleet, betting as they go. A variety of zealous politicians have tried to stamp out the 'gambling evil' but a bet's a bet in Sydney.

On Darling Point, above the 18-footers clubhouse, is one of Sydney's most beautiful churches ... St Marks. The foundation stone was laid in 1848 at one of the highest sites on the ridge of the point. The Gothic-styled church was opened in 1852 and a slender and graceful spire added in 1875.

The church has the sailing clubhouse behind it in Double Bay and stands facing the Cruising Yacht Club in Rushcutters Bay. This is the heartland of the ocean racers, the governing body for one of the world's great races, the Sydney to Hobart classic. Since 1945 the race has been held on the demanding 680 sea mile course. On Boxing Bay the Harbour goes berserk, a nightmare day for the Coast Guard and the Water Police as sightseers in ferries, powerboats, speedboats, yachts and even skiffs and windsurfers form a floating gallery. Balloons, streamers, flags and beer cans ring the fleet as it circles waiting for the starting gun. Then there's that magical sight of the maxi-yachts racing for the honour

Below: Some are bottomless, some topless, some both. Anything goes...it's Lady Bay, one of Sydney's two official nudist beaches. **Right:** Point Piper, where Sydney's rich live...including Robert and Susan Sangster who paid $6 million for their summer home on the water...that white Spanish-arched home with a lot of green and a, temporarily, empty pool. **Bottom:** The better Vaucluse mansions, naturally, have a Rolls-Royce in the garage.

of being first through the Heads; crews stretching every sinew, sails testing every stitch.

Away from the glamour of the yacht clubs, and the splendour of the harbour, is Taylor Square with its grim past. Until 100 years ago this was the outskirts of the city centre...a ghetto of huts and shanties, populated equally by down-and-outs and rats. In the plague at the turn of the century much of the area was torn down as the rats were burnt out. The Darlinghurst Gaol in Forbes Street was the scene of the last public hangings. Here the Strangler, hangman Alexander Green, strung up the luckless convicts. As if it weren't bad enough to face death in the morning, the condemned men had to crouch on all fours all night in a small cell cut into the sandstone walls.

The city has its sordid past. And its sordid present. Early in 1984 it became fashionable among European journalists to write about Australia

and especially Sydney. John Pilger, the celebrated Sydney journalist now based in London, wrote a column extolling the virtues of Sydney for the *New Statesman*. Simon Hoggett, of the *Observer* in Fleet Street, described Kings Cross as a mild, red light area — 'the kind of thing Walt Disney might do if he were to create a Viceland'. Hoggett skipped across the surface of the Cross; saw the mild passing street parade and the handful of luring leering lights and walked on. The Cross is much more — and much less. It is exploitative, it is sad and it is cheap. There are nightclubs and coffee bars where heroin is almost as easy to buy as capuccino. There are teenagers on the run from school and home and

turning to the Wayside Chapel for relief. The girls are driven from their streetside patches to others; if prostitution threatens real estate values it is moved on. The Cross, despite attempts to dress it up, is a tart. Early last century, though, it was the most fashionable residential area in Sydney. The breathtaking view from Potts Point gave rise to mansions. Then it was Woolloomooloo Hill. It became Queens Cross in 1879 and Kings Cross in 1905 to celebrate King Edward VII.

Much livelier, safer and more entertaining is the Haymarket end of town. It may be the home of Sydney's derelicts but is still more savoury than the Cross. It's much easier on the nerves and the pocket to be cajoled out of 20 cents than mugged for a wallet. The Haymarket holds the Sydney Entertainment Centre, spartanly concrete though it is, and the lively Chinatown.

Nightlife in Sydney is not the breath-sapping, exhilarating ordeal it is in Manhattan or Paris. But then they don't have the days Sydney does...

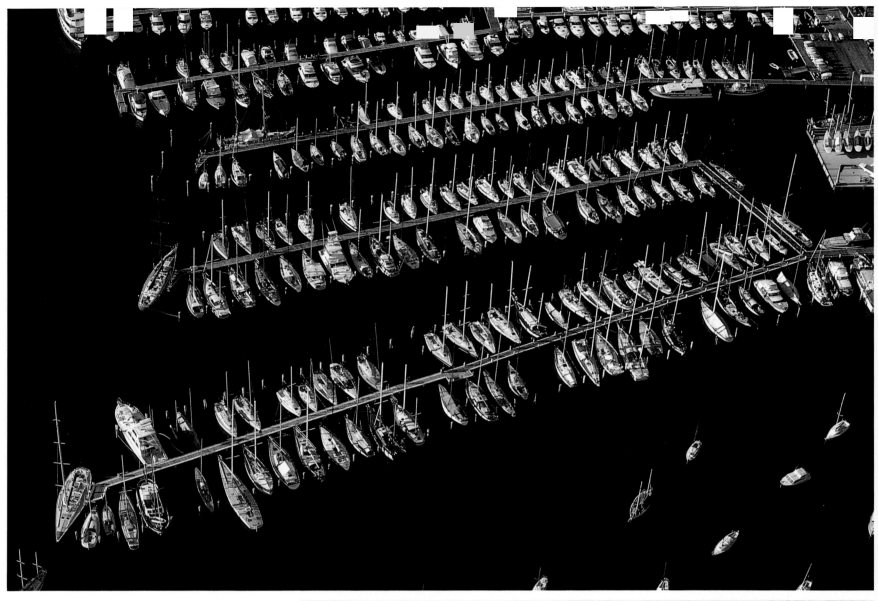

Top: The arms of the marina at the Cruising Yacht Club in Rushcutters Bay are almost full on a Tuesday afternoon. But at the weekend it's like a deserted drive-in theatre.
Right: The lakes of Centennial Park are home to a rich variety of waterfowl and wildlife...including eels. **Opposite:** New South Head Road winds its way down from Kings Cross and the City in Double Bay, Sydney's exclusive shopping address.

Left: On a Thursday afternoon, the Harbour is uncluttered off Point Piper with a handful of yachts making the most of it.
Below: Watsons Bay and in the foreground, Camp Cove.

Left: Royal Sydney Golf Club and the most manicured greens in New South Wales.
Below: There's little green left here... Paddington, once a working class suburb with its humble terraces, has been redecorated as an upmarket colony for photographers, models, their Beagles and Great Danes. But the winding, one-way streets haven't changed...

Opposite: Jersey Road runs off Oxford Street to form the Paddington-Woollahra 'boundary'. On the corner of Jersey Road, the Light Brigade Hotel, with its bricks, tiles and distinctive styling, is a classic example of the street corner pub. **Below:** The day the water police and the coastguard dread ... Boxing Day. And thousands of small boats, often with unskilled or unsober skippers, jostle and push to be part of the action: the start of the Sydney to Hobart classic.

THE WORKWAYS

BUILT ON bullock tracks, forced up hills and to cross rivers, creeks and the harbour, Sydney travel is no delight. A succession of State Governments has stalled and dithered over extending freeways or building second harbour crossings. But Sydney, despite being a car city, is still relatively well serviced by trains, buses and ferries.

The cars choke the Cahill Expressway on the Harbour Bridge morning and evening; they queue in the north at the Spit Bridge and in the south at Tom Uglys Bridge. They crawl along Parramatta Road and limp along the Pacific Highway or Victoria Road. But they get there ... slow or not, Sydney wouldn't be without its cars. Sadly, the ferry potential of the city has never been developed fully. The oddest corners of the city are serviced by private ferry. From tiny Thames Street wharf in Balmain's Mort Bay a ferry takes off twice a morning, dropping passengers considerately at McMahons Point on the lower North Shore before plodding on to Circular Quay. But these runs are few. Manly has its ferries and hydrofoils and the croaking, creaking antiquated ferries labour up the Lane Cove River to Hunters Hill and Woolwich. But mass ferry or hydrofoil services are limited. It certainly was in pre-Depression days and before the opening of the Bridge when even business tycoons left their cars at a wharf and 'had their chance to daydream on the way to the office aboard the ferries, then walk leisurely up Pitt Street to their offices near the Stock Exchange, the centre of Sydney's business scene'.

The roads, unlike the ferries, are reaching breaking point. Every Sydney driver knows 'the back way'. But the sneaky little routes that bypass the main routes are becoming as clogged as the arteries themselves. It's not surprising. The city was developed and expanded on bullock tracks. Darling Point, one of Sydney's more celebrated addresses today, was, for example, an outpost of the city in the middle of last century. It was regarded then as a bit far out of town. But by the 1880s it had a metalled roof and a fair sprinkling of mansions. Today massive high-rise blocks loom against the skyline. Where roads were developed for 20 or 30 mansions, thousands of residents park their cars and scramble from the side streets on to New South Head Road each morning for the bumper-to-bumper crawl into the city.

It was easy in the days when a few horse and carts shared the crossroads or even when motorised transport came to town and 30km/h was a daring speed. Then crossroads such as the Five Ways at Paddington, the Seven Ways at North Bondi and the Nine Ways at Kingsford could be navigated easily. Today it's like the Champs Elysées peak hour or the Indianapolis 500. Cars scream through the intersections or, in the case of Nine Ways, the roundabout, at limit-defying speeds, daring other drivers to stick out their noses. Buses, early in 1984, were

From Vaucluse to Mascot...the coastal strip of the Eastern Suburbs. A network of avenues, streets, crescents and cul-de-sacs all feed into a handful of city-bound roads.

Preceding: At 6.30 am the traffic is already building up on the southern approaches to the Harbour Bridge.

Below: The commuter rush is over. In the last of the evening light, the ferries sit back at Circular Quay and relax. Two or three more runs tonight and then a few hours' sleep before it all begins again at dawn.
Right: The feeder lines at Central Railway are almost deserted on a Sunday. Their busy time will come at rush hour tomorrow.
Bottom: Dusk, but the Harbour Bridge rush is still on . . . five lanes north and three south to meet the city exodus.

given complete run of the road. It became illegal for other motorists to prevent them changing lanes. That was an unwritten law Sydney drivers had known about for many years ... don't defy the buses. They could stop on the left and move out across two, or even three, lanes at will.

The Parramatta Road, for a long time the main western road in and out of the city, was the original historic route to Parramatta. The oldest highway in Australia it is never still, even on Sunday morning when any self-respecting motorist is sleeping in. It was built in 1794 ... a sheet of red dust in summer and a bog in winter. In 1806 the Government ordered drivers of empty coaches to stock up with bricks from the brickworks near Central Railway. They were to drop these in the giant potholes as they went west. Today the Parramatta Road has a different kind of pitfall ... the ugly row after row of car yards, a monument to the motoring society Sydney has become. Neon signs fight with streamers

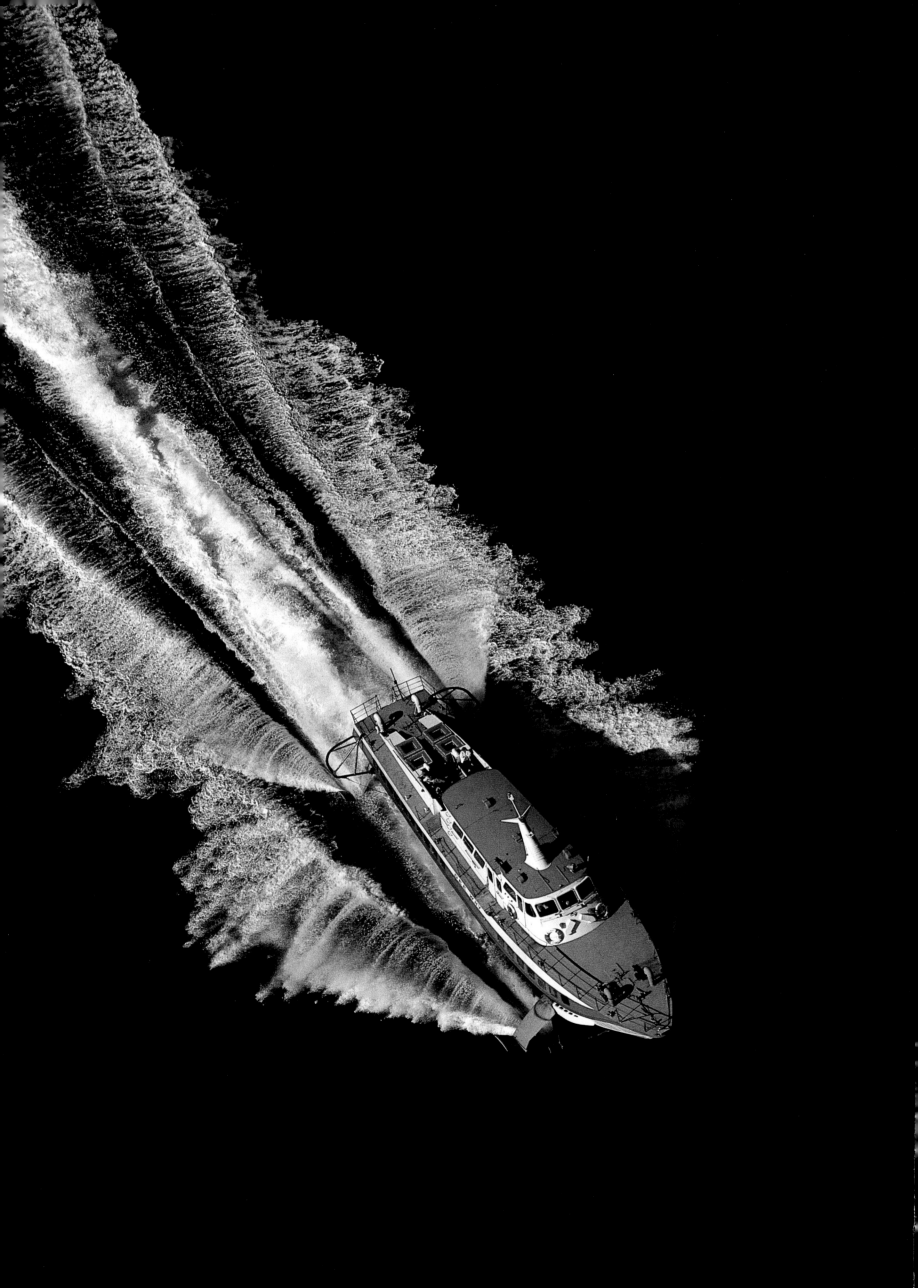

and bunting for attention; potential buyers crawl along looking for a good deal, trucks pass them cursing and hooting on horns which would do a transatlantic steamer justice. The Parramatta Road is not for the timid.

The Pacific Highway is little better. It may be easier on the eye but it's just as tough on the nerves. Most roads in Sydney have reached their limit. And the many bridges which cross the rivers and extensions of the harbour are feeling the pinch, too. Some are more than 100 years old, built before Daimler Benz put their first car on the road. The Gladesville Bridge between Gladesville and Five Dock was opened on February 1, 1881; the Iron Cove Bridge in 1882. The Iron Cove Bridge carries much of the traffic too weary and battle-scarred to face another Harbour Bridge crawl. But a series of State Governments has faced and postponed the prospect of a second harbour crossing. Everyone wants a second crossing; no-one wants it in their own back yard.

THE WATERWAYS

THE ROLLING swell of the South Pacific Ocean dies at South Head. The promontory, nearly 5km long, rises from water 10-20 fathoms deep, a series of abrupt sandstone cliffs as rugged as a Rugby front row.

Like the cliffs of Dover the sandstone face of South Head is a landmark. The smell of the first beer for the dry sailor who has pounded his way up the coast. The waves, the swell, the gales are all cut down to

Three men in a boat ... well, nearly in. The crew of the *Bradmill* out on the trapeze in Sydney's unique 18-footer racing. Every Sunday the 18-footers set out from Double Bay, accompanied by a ferryload of unofficial gamblers. The boats get lighter each year; the betting gets heavier. **Over:** The other great race on Sydney Harbour ... the annual ferry boat clash ... a handicap event with the older and smaller ferries given a head start. It's still anybody's race here as the fleet charges back to the finishing line.

size at South Head. Inside the Harbour the water is soft and smooth. Peaceful little bays on the inner side of South Head ignore the battering around the point on the eastern face.

Lady Bay, where nude sunbathers watch the ripples; Watson's Bay, where fish lovers eat at Doyle's on the waterfront and admire the gentle flow of the slight waves; Rose Bay, where windsurfers skate across a millpond. None of these bays and their visitors seems to realise that only a thin peninsula stands between them and the open ocean. South Head is divided into Inner and Outer South Head. Outer South Head is an elbow on the peninsula jutting defiantly to the ocean. Between there and

the actual entrance lies The Gap, notorious for its suicide victims. The thin strand of land behind The Gap, barely half a kilometre wide, prevents the ocean flooding into Sydney Harbour.

One of the great harbours in the world began life as a laconic entry in the journal of Captain Cook. Having landed at Botany Bay he sailed north, stopping at Broken Bay, the mouth of the Hawkesbury River. Sighting the gap between North and South Head, and the expanse of Middle Harbour, Cook noted unromantically, 'there appears to be safe anchorage which I call Port Jackson'.

From a handful of houses on the South Head ridge is one of the most beautiful views in Sydney. They are not even the most expensive homes or the most lavish but for a few moments each morning and again in the

Below: Port Hacking, with its sheltered bays and calm moorings, is home to thousands of motor boats and yachts. **Right**: On the edge of South Head at Dover Heights the houses in Douglas Parade and Wentworth Street cling to the lip of the land.

evening they see the sun rise on the rim of the ocean and watch it set over the west, the Bridge, the city and the Harbour. They see that peculiar rose pink turn to red and purple and fade into an inkiness as the sun vanishes behind the Blue Mountains. There is, from The Gap, a staggering view where an ocean is brought to its knees and behind, in the safety of the Harbour, windsurfers flirt with a breeze barely capable of moving water. There are other views in Sydney, even more spectacular scenes, but few people are lucky enough to see the fury on one side and the calmness on the other.

It's a vast harbour, the shoreline measuring 240km with its 107 bays and coves. The average width of the main harbour is 1.6km and in more than half the harbour the minimum depth at low tide is 10 metres. The average rise and fall of the harbour is 1.6 metres; the depth between the Heads at the ocean entrance is 25 metres.

These are the cold facts. Pilots need to know them; the Maritime Services Board cherish them; sailors and container ship crews bear them in mind.

But they don't tell the real story of Sydney Harbour: the unrivalled joy of watching a suspiciously old ferry chug up to a creaking wharf. Of seeing a casual, bearded deckhand expertly lasso the pylon and throw the gangplank on to the jetty. Of that stomach-turning moment like being on the Luna Park roller-coaster when you're midway down the gangplank and the boat hiccups. Just for a moment there's a chill … the boat's slipping, the gangplank's falling and you're going head over elbow into the Harbour. It never happens.

You can be on a yacht glistening out of the Harbour to cruise up the coast at sunrise; on a power cruiser arrogantly carving a wake as it races the yachts at the start of the Sydney to Hobart yachting classic or sitting in a dinghy fishing and cursing as the hydrofoil rocks you off balance. To taste the Harbour is to taste Sydney.

The blocks of flats that crowd on to the shoreline like front-row spectators at a rock concert; or the land-greedy mansions of Point Piper which have cost as much as $6 million, leer hungrily at the Harbour.

But in Pittwater they have a connoisseur's eye, appreciatively looking through ironbarks and ghost gums at the gentle stretches of the Pittwater basin. In the built-up regions of Careel Bay and Newport, or across on Scotland Island where builders are making impossible demands on steep sites, they take the occasional koalas and possums and flying foxes for granted. The Pittwater waterway is more relaxed. The ocean gave up work at Barrenjoey and the waters of the Pittwater are enjoying their retirement.

Life is easier on Pittwater. The ferries are smaller and a little less frisky, dinghies are still available for hire. Even the yachts which sail out of the Royal Prince Alfred Yacht Club at Newport aren't quite as overbearing as the Harbour yachts. They're less aggressive, more liable to give a wide berth to the houseboats and cabin cruisers they know are in the hands of once-a-year captains. And no-one is quite as keen to topple into the water here. Sharks are a rarity in the Harbour but they are spotted in Pittwater. And the giant jellyfish which trail through the water may not be deadly but they're not reassuring. The beaches of Pittwater are unspoilt ... even where the parkland surrenders to residential areas. After Europeans arrived in Sydney, but before Pittwater was opened up, casuarina forests grew down to the shoreline at the now wealthy suburb of Church Point. They gave way to mangrove swamps as the foreshore slid into the sea. The mangroves in turn gave way to the developers. But unlike Sydney Harbour where vast areas of waterfront land have been scarred by apartment blocks, the coastal rim of Pittwater has been developed gently.

The western wall of Pittwater is the limit of the giant Ku-Ring-Gai Chase national park. Originally this was the home of the first true Sydneysiders, the Kuring-gai tribesmen who lived on the shores of Broken Bay and west to the Hawkesbury. Where the bluntly forceful cliffs of the Chase fall into Pittwater and round the inlets into the Hawkesbury they lived off the rich sea pickings and the land.

In turn the valleys and alluvial flats of the Hawkesbury supported the

Farms feeding on the rich alluvial soil run down to the banks of the Hawkesbury River. From the hills above Wiseman's Ferry a lone speedboat curls in the river.

early colonists. Giant gatherings of quail, wild ducks and black swan once flooded the Hawkesbury; today it's oyster farmers and the water skiers. A series of rivers, as far inland as Crookwell and the Wollondilly River give rise to the Hawkesbury. The river proper begins at Grose Wold where the Nepean River joins the Grose to become the quiet moving, murmuring stretch called the Hawkesbury, after an early Minister of Trade and Plantations.

For many Sydneysiders the Hawkesbury is Wiseman's Ferry where the ferry punts still rasp their way across on iron cables. Above Wiseman's Ferry, on Hawkins Lookout, the water skiers leave tracks like ants crossing a patch of spilt sugar, carving a lacework pattern on the broad reaches. The river flats with their rich, loam soil cry out to be used. The ferry was established in 1827...cattle were threepence a head. Today it's the picnickers who are herded into rows in their cars and carried across to the northern side.

Houseboats and cabin cruisers trickle through the Hawkesbury...

steered by men with the hands of amateurs but the hearts of a Cook. Serious sailors scoff but it's as exciting as blue water sailing to the men at the helm.

The Hawkesbury is the lazy river, moving through parkland and grazing land, relatively untouched by development. The Parramatta, from its beginnings in western life in November, 1788, grew in another direction. Houses crowd its banks, factories spill waste in it, bottles float in it, cans sink in it. The Parramatta passes through the heartland of suburban Sydney.

The feverish little creek that becomes the river begins at Northmead, west of Parramatta the second oldest settlement in Australia. It was along the convenient Parramatta River that Governor Phillip travelled with a small boatload of people to select the site for development. At Rose Hill, near the well-developed racecourse, huts were thrown up. George Street is now a thriving shopping centre with high-rise office blocks. But it began with a wharf at its foot. From a moderate beginning in its upper reaches the Parramatta winds its way down to Long Nose Point on the western side of Balmain. In the broad sound approaching Long Nose Point from the west the Parramatta and Lane Cove Rivers meet, surrendering to become the Harbour.

In the years between Governor Phillip's beginnings and the 1950s the Parramatta River grew filthier. Silverwater became a virtual cesspool. Here, at the meeting point of the Duck River and the Parramatta, oily wastes and chemical residues poured into the water. The Clean Waters Act of 1970 and action by the industries have slowly cleaned up the vast waterway. It took time. In 1971 no species of fish were recorded in Duck River and only two freshwater species ... and they were both dead ... were found below the weir at Parramatta. By 1976 twelve species had returned to the upper Parramatta. The river will never be as clean as it was in 1788 but the damage has been stemmed. From the air the river is a clay colour with the wash from the banks. Yet it still attracts water skiers and cabin cruisers.

But the gathering place for cruisers, speedboats — for all varieties of power boats — is Port Hacking, named after First Fleet pilot Henry Hacking who had heard of rumours 'of a large river south of Botany Bay'. Motor boat clubs flourish in Port Hacking; large, even ostentatious, homes boast little jetties with cabin cruisers rather than yachts. The inlets are studded with safe anchorages. Port Hacking, even after 200 years of dedicated fishing, is still an angler's dream. The southern arm of the bay is almost deserted; pockets of development have been allowed but the majority of the sweep of the bay belongs to the Royal National Park, Australia's oldest, being dedicated in 1872, and the second oldest national park in the world after the US Yellowstone National Park. From Audley, the innermost part of Port Hacking to the Point which curves around to shield the entrance to the bay from the southerly swells, Port Hacking is dominated by houses running to the water to the north and ghost gums dropping their leaves in the ripples on the south.

Right: The seawall at Botany is a popular spot for weekend fishermen.

Below: The 'islands' of Sylvania Waters, west of the Captain Cook Bridge crossing the Georges River, are home to more than 100 families. In the upper left is Murray Island, linked to Sylvania by Bogan Avenue. Opposite is Barcoo Island, with Tuross Avenue as its bridge. And in the foreground, part of the near circular James Cook Island, held to the 'mainland' by Warrego Avenue.

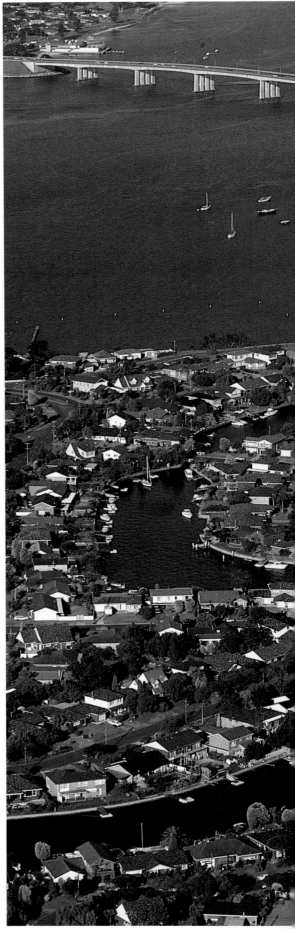

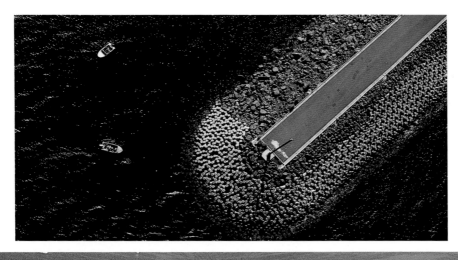

The islands of Sydney...

Industry and history; gas tanks and jazz bands. Somehow they manage to live side by side in Sydney. The islands of Sydney Harbour, unlike those of Pittwater and the Hawkesbury, are not residential. But Berry Island, perhaps because it is no longer a true island, is the temporary home of jazz bands once a month. Hundreds of jazz lovers (well, admirers) crowd on to the island and its narrow peninsula connecting it to the mainland. They wallow in the sun and drink red wine from the cask. Only jazz musicians and their followers

Balls Head, jutting out into the Harbour past the BP tanks, no longer ends in an island. The mud flats were reclaimed, linking it to the shore. But it's still a picnic hideaway only minutes from the city.

Following page: Fort Denison, or Pinchgut, Sydney's most famous island, with its Martello Tower which was to stand between Sydney and the invading Russians!

seem to have the peculiar stamina to survive a day in the summer heat drinking the strong cheap wine that turns sour and dry by mid-afternoon. The trumpets become strained and the saxophones falter but they see it out. Berry Island is named after North Sydney pioneer Alexander Berry who had a causeway built. In the 1960s the mud flats were reclaimed and filled in, creating a natural reserve. Alongside the 'island', the BP oil tanks clutter up Balls Head on one side and on the other the western shore of Gore Cove has been sliced into sandstone cupboards to cater for more oil tanks. Somehow the lower north shore harbour rises above these industrial scars. The arm of the Harbour is too beautiful to be blighted by one or two small boils.

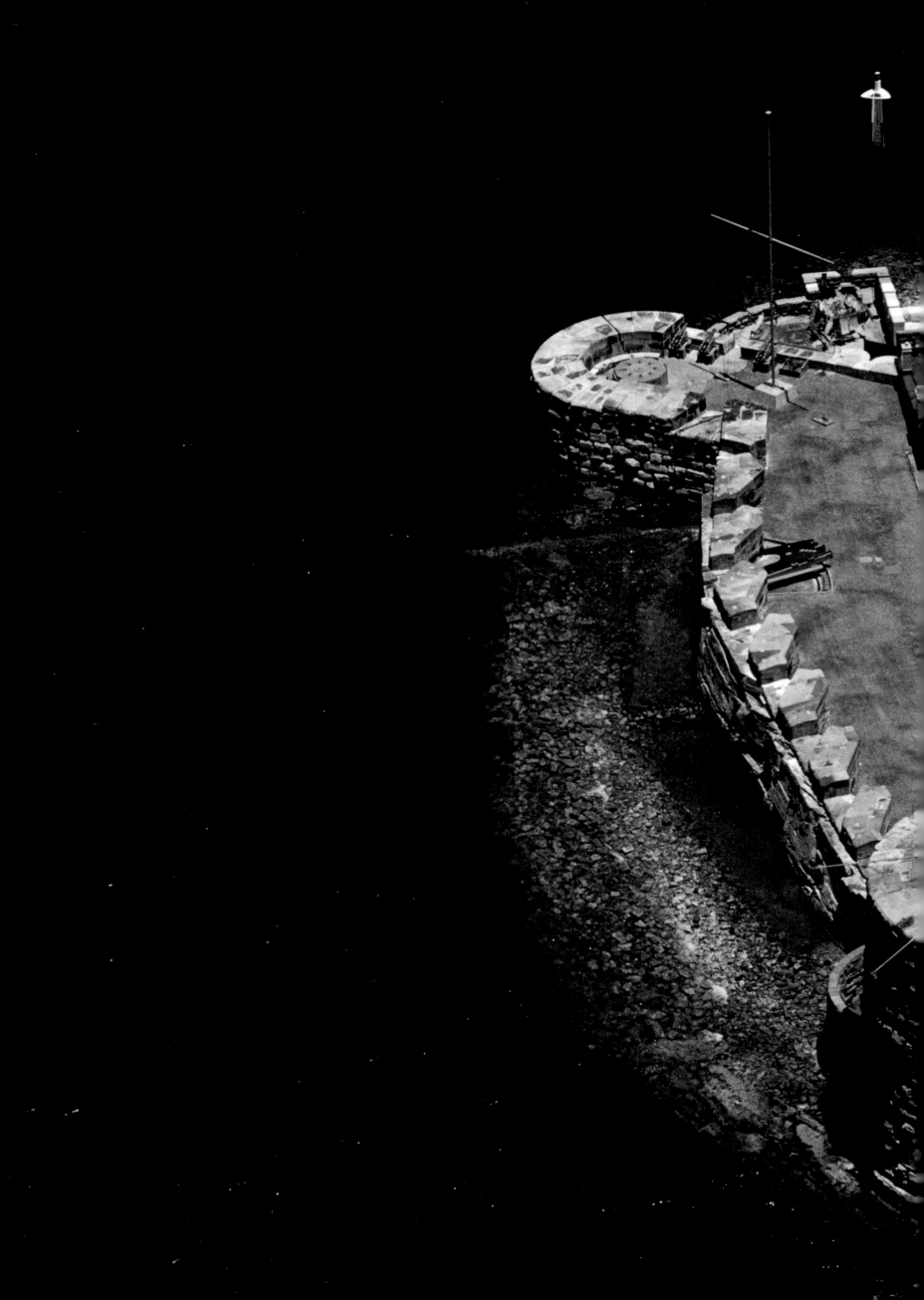

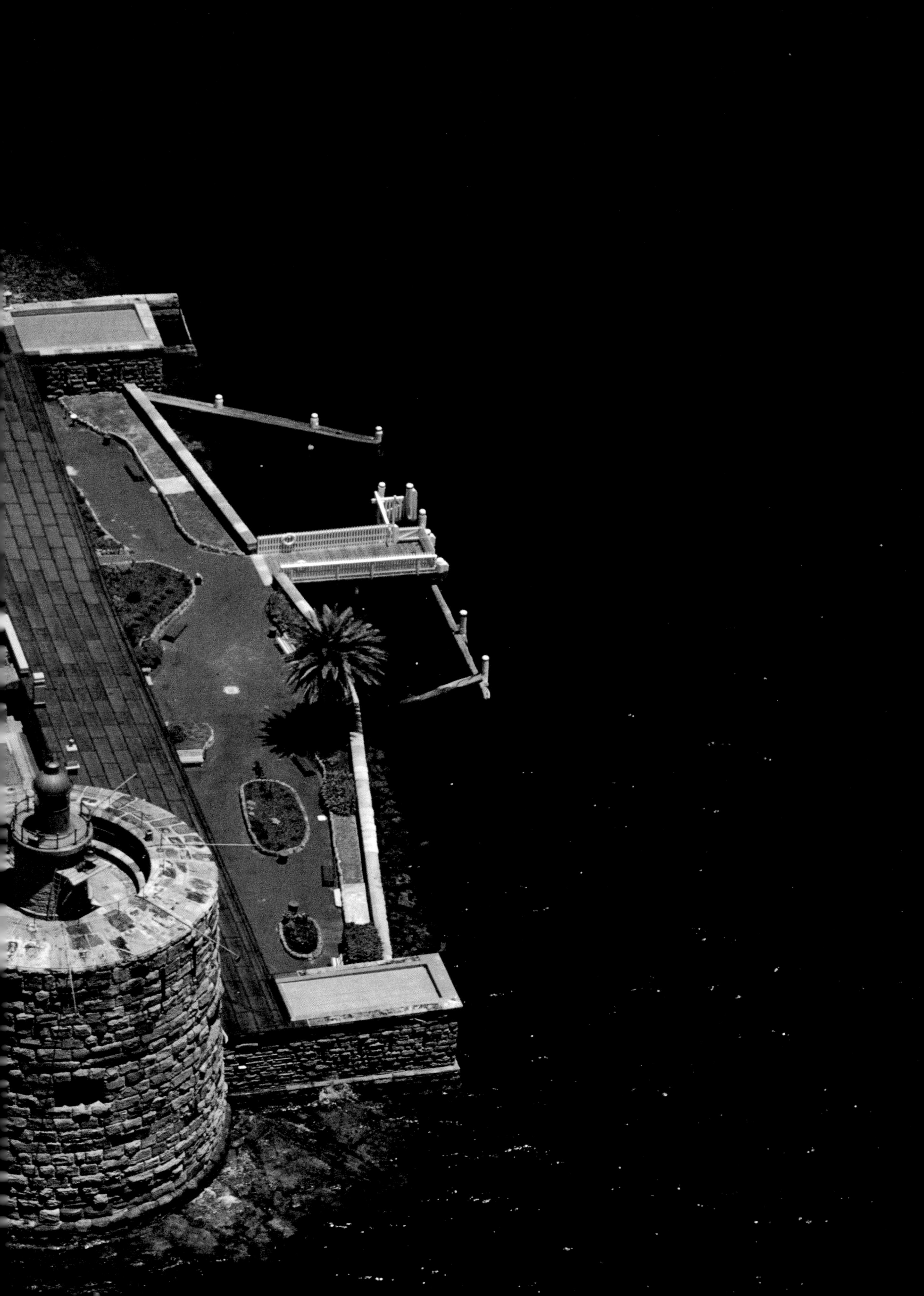

Left: The Cockatoo Island dockyard, an island marred by industry. **Bottom:** The island again ... a few brave trees struggling in a sea of sheet metal and docks. **Below:** Birkenhead Point, the sail-in shopping complex in the inner west. The marina and seven-day shopping centre are booming. **Over:** A 1984 view from the lower North Shore taken by Leo Meier from the Haye estate, now the site of the North Sydney Girls High School. **Over:** The same view from a balloon ... in 1904.

The island the tourists and most Sydneysiders see and admire is Pinchgut ... Fort Denison, to be accurate but it's far less dramatic. More or less off the Opera House with its low stone walls and its Martello Tower, Pinchgut is an obvious landmark. And the name? Take your pick ... navy men insist it is simply a reference to the narrowing of the channel ... a 'pinching of the gut'. Romantics insist it refers to the effect of a diet of bread and water fed to the convicts. At the first criminal court held in Australia ... February 8, 1788, convict Thomas Hill spent a week on the island restricted to ships' biscuits and water. Nine years later another convict Morgan, suffered a much

less lenient fate. He was hanged in chains on a gibbet and left there to dry and blacken in the sun for three years.

The Martello Tower was built during the Crimean War when Sydney feared the Russian fleet would come south. The fevered building of emplacements on Bradley's Head was matched in the Harbour ... the tower was built on Pinchgut as a gun-mounting, and three 32-pounders were installed. They cannot be taken away without destroying the fort, so Pinchgut still exists as it did in 1856.

Not far from Pinchgut is Garden Island, like Berry, not a true island. Before World War II it

Below: Goat Island off Balmain...the depot for the Maritime Services Board. Unlike Cockatoo it has been preserved as well as utilised. **Bottom:** Shark Island off Rose Bay...the first island to greet a ship coming through the heads, it has been preserved as part of Sydney Harbour National Park.

was separated from Potts Point by a 300-metre channel. But from 1940 to 1945, the sea bed was built up to create a dockyard. Today, with the sweeping sails of the Opera House and the coathanger of the Harbour Bridge, Garden Island with its fascinatingly ugly sprawl of giant cranes and steel towers stands as another, less pretty example, of man's engineering skill. Strangely it is so ugly it's almost attractive. On an early Sunday morning, guiding an old ketch away from the Cruising Yacht Club and out of Rushcutters Bay the sunrise catches Garden Island. No men are at work; no clanging echoes across the water. Just a still series of mechanical statues.

Cockatoo Island is unrecognisable today from the time of the First Fleet. Then it was a sturdy lump of rock, covered with tall redgums and the home of a giant flock of sulphur-crested cockatoos. Today it is the biggest shipyard in the Harbour. The largest island and the biggest eyesore, even though much of the shipbuilding work has been transferred to Garden Island. In the passage between Cockatoo and the Drummoyne Peninsula lie Spectacle Island and Snapper Island, used as a navy armaments depot and a scouts training depot respectively.

When the First Fleet landed in Sydney three goats had survived the long journey. Hand-me-down

history says Goat Island was their resting place, with its meagre supply of grass, while the First Fleeters set up shop. There's no hard evidence to support the theory but as a story it's just fine. Today Goat Island is operated by the Maritime Services Board as a repair shipyard. It is also the home of the Port's Fire Brigade.

The first islands to greet an incoming ship are Clarke and Shark, the often confused islands off Double Bay (Clarke) and Rose Bay (Shark). Both are part of the Sydney Harbour National Park … there to be enjoyed by the city. Clarke is slightly smaller and steeper; Shark has gentle rolling slopes. Both are available to picnickers and a summer's day gives a taste of the Harbour even yachtsmen envy.

Rodd Island, in Iron Cove, is Crown land. The island is named after the Rodd family of Drummoyne and on Rodd Point, on the mainland at Iron Cove, a large stone cross marks the family mausoleum which was carved out of huge rock. These are the islands of Sydney Harbour. In Pittwater, Scotland Island has virtually become a suburb with ferries for the commuters and even a road for weekend builders to drive their timber and bricks around. Dangar Island, off Brooklyn in the Hawkesbury, is similar although the houses tend to be for the genuine weekend retreater.

There are other islands in Brisbane Waters and Hawkesbury, each with unique history. But Sydney's overlooked island is Lord Howe, administered by the City of Sydney, yet 600km off the coastline, in the heart of the South Pacific Ocean.

The Bare Island museum and fort, linked to La Perouse by a thread of land, have been preserved as an historic site.

THE WEST

THAT SPRAWLING part of Sydney called the West. It begins at historic Balmain and runs past the equally historic Parramatta, out to the foothills of the Blue Mountains. It doesn't have beaches; it doesn't have sea views. There are no Centennial Parks, no ferries, no coastal breezes calming the summer sun.

The city school children refer to their 'inland' peers as Westies. It's

Groomed gardens and healthy trees on the fringe of Blacktown in Sydney's west, a garden pocket in the spread of new housing. **Over:** Throughout the west, above-ground swimming pools dot the back yards. The temperature in the west, unrelieved by coastal breezes, can climb degrees higher than in the east in summer.

said derogatively and it's meant. And yet the West *is* Sydney. The coastline and the Harbour, the Opera House and the Bridge: they're the trappings, the logos. Heartland Sydney is around Auburn. Even, ironically, around the massive Rookwood cemetery. As the population grew it had to go west, forced by the natural boundaries to the north, south and east which prohibited expansion. In population terms, Auburn is the central point of Sydney. To live in Sydney and never taste the flavour of the West is not to know the city.

The pride of suburban living, the inter-relationship between neighbours, the feel of a street, the shopping village pockets and the giant

Preceding: A new settlement springs up near Penrith. The urban heart of Sydney gradually moves to the west ... the only direction left to expand.

Above: Campbelltown, a satellite city and Sydney's fastest growing region.

complexes of Roselands and Westpoint. Sydney lives differently away from the sea. Swimming pools, for example, have a new significance. In the eastern suburbs and the south they're a social symbol ... 'we can afford the ocean *and* a pool'. In the West they're almost a necessity. When it's a sizzling 32C degrees on the coast and city workers are complaining about the heat as they leave their air-conditioned offices at lunchtime it can be 38C degrees or worse in the West. A wall of heat walks down Church Street, Parramatta. It goes slowly, forming around you as you walk. Inland Australia is sending out a warning. The dry heat is worse in some ways than the rare humid days Sydney endures. The heat chokes in your throat. Breathing is improbably painful. On days like this the West falls into its pools ... sculptured pools of slate and marine-varnished wood or humble, plastic, above ground pools. It doesn't matter ... the water is cool.

The wonderful old suburb of Hunters Hill... Sydney's smallest... runs away from the Gladesville Bridge and out into the Lane Cove River. Some of Sydney's most magnificent homes are in this pocket suburb which is not quite in the north, not quite in the west.

For much of Sydney the West means a crawl to Liverpool on a day's outing to Camden or the Bowral areas. Or a cruise down Parramatta Road checking out the car yards; an occasional trip to the bulk buying, cheap selling factories and warehouses. But one of Sydney's most beautiful homes is in the West; some of the city's rarest old churches and graveyards are in the West; the quaintest suburb is in the inner West; the true delicatessens of Italy are in the West. In one corner of Leichhardt is a delicatessen, an Italian bread shop and coffee bean boutique selling flavours and smells the ritzy suburb of Double Bay can't match. And it's half the price!

The West is a sprawling mass of people living in relative harmony. The various Lebanese sects who manage to kill each other by the hundreds on any given day in Beirut pass by each other in the streets of Punchbowl; the Vietnamese who brought violence to Cabramatta when

It's a fair haul from Ryde to the sea. But when you've got the Victoria Road swimming pool on your doorstep it doesn't seem to matter. The pool is run by the Ryde Municipal Council who also keeps the grass trimmed for sunbaking. **Over:** Backyard market gardens in West Pennant Hills, enough land to go round for a home and a profitable sideline.

they first arrived have opted for the Australian way of existence. It may be indifference but at least it's peaceful. Sydney is one of the most cosmopolitan cities in the world ... represented by every colour and race imaginable. But on a fine day, the local Nazi party is flat out raising a crowd of 200 to listen to its hatred. In a city of three million, just 200 feel inclined to turn up ... it says volumes for the nature of the Sydney and the West that it lives with itself.

A gradual westward tour of this major area of Sydney proves that the West has so much more to offer than discount furniture and second-hand cars.

Balmain In many ways the perfect Sydney suburb. It gave birth to a Prime Minister (Billy Hughes) and State Premier (Neville Wran) an Olympic champion (Dawn Fraser) and the controversial Governor-General, Sir John Kerr, son of a local boilermaker. More church spires

A multi-million dollar home with a difference ... a bullring, four waterfalls, a trout pool and a helipad. The home, built of three million bricks, is called Notre Dame by Frenchman Emmanuel Margolin. On the outskirts of Penrith he is creating a unique 'chateau'.

Parramatta Gaol ... the maximum security prison housing some of Australia's most dangerous criminals.

wind up through the trees of Balmain, than the population could need. A factory ... the Colgate-Palmolive plant ... has lived on the waterfront for more than 60 years, magnificent old terraces and Federation bungalows share the streets with blocks of flats. Balmain is all things. In Louisa Road, Birchgrove, a narrow road housing Porsches, a Maserati and Jaguars parked carelessly to straddle the footpath and the street, rock stars have chosen to buy the art nouveau or wrought iron decorated houses. They could afford the much pricier suburbs but the feeling of Birchgrove/Balmain has a pulling power of its own.

Balmain is part of the inner city municipality of Leichhardt, sharing the aldermen with Glebe, Rozelle, Annandale and Lilyfield. Leichhardt is one of Sydney's many Little Italys. Unlike New York, where there is one well defined Little Italy, every part of Sydney that has a pizza bar and an espresso machine seems to earn the name. Darlinghurst fights

Near the heart of the city, Randwick Racecourse is headquarters for Sydney racing. The horses mill in the mounting yard before going to the starting barrier. Randwick stages the Sydney Cup and AJC Derby among other feature events. **Above:** Canterbury Racecourse in the west is another of Sydney's four major tracks. As well, dog and trotting tracks keep the TAB ticking over.

for the privilege but Leichhardt is the true titleholder ... with its superb pasta houses, fresh bread shops and the coffee shops that fill the streets with an intoxicating smell. Middle-aged Italian men, stand on the footpath arrogantly assessing each woman as she walks by; la dolce vita. Balmain and Glebe are a magnificent record of old homes and buildings. So too is ...

Strathfield, one of the most attractive suburbs of Sydney, with magnificent old homes and gardens. Strathfield began life as part of Liberty Plains, a farming area set up to supply the growing town. The actual area of Strathfield was named Redmyre until 1885. Gentlemen's residences began being built in the 1870s and 1880s when the land proved not productive enough for farming and Sydney was beginning to feel adventurous enough to live in the area. Albert Road became the

centre of Strathfield and today is still a monument to those days of last century. Albert House, sprawled over two giant blocks, was built in 1890-91, just before the economic crash of 1893. The Samuel Hordern family was able to snap it up in 1901 and renamed it Tuxedo. Next door is Jesmond, formerly the home of Washington H. Soul. Today much of Strathfield has been retained as stately old homes surrounded by manicured gardens. The neighbouring suburb of Homebush is the home of the main Sydney abattoirs. But originally it was the magnificent estate of D'Arcy Wentworth.

Concord, to the north, also has its share of beautiful estates. And one of Sydney's most magnificent homes is on the eastern shore of Yaralla Bay. Scottish investor and shipping tycoon Thomas Walker built Yaralla in the 1860s, surrounded by the best estate parkland in the city. His

The Thomas Walker Convalescent Hospital at Rocky Point...a large mansion facing the Parramatta River, overlooking the 2000 metre rowing course. The elder brother to Yaralla house, this is one of Sydney's most magnificent homes. Inside the grounds of the Thomas Walker Hospital is a small but fascinating museum.

The Yaralla home on the eastern shore of Yaralla Bay, Concord, was built by Scottish investor and shipping tycoon Thomas Walker in the 1860s. His daughter survived him and lived in the home until her death in 1937 when it became a convalescent hospital.

daughter survived him and lived in Yaralla until her death in 1937 when the mansion became the Dame Eadith Walker Convalescent Hospital. It stands white and proud on the headland, overlooking the official 2000-metre rowing course on the Parramatta River. On the facing headland stands the Thomas Walker Convalescent Hospital, larger but not as magnificent. Inside the grounds of the hospital is a small but fascinating historical museum.

Marrickville, to the south and east of Strathfield, is a perfect example of multi-racial Sydney. Greek, Italian, Turkish and Yugoslav communities exist side by side. The Greeks and the Turks never tire of fighting one another in contentious Cyprus; in Sydney their bitterness doesn't seem as valid. A Thai temple in Stanmore celebrates the Buddhist festival of Songkran each year and the incense and food stalls in the street give the area an unusual annual flavour.

The district covers a number of land grants made between 1794 and 1802. Until the 1930s it remained a farming area. Then settlers began to move in, at first to establish market gardens and then to build homes. The development of Marrickville had begun. But it was the immediate period after World War II that saw today's Marrickville boom. It was a cheap area to buy into and the migrants flooding in from war-torn Europe gravitated to Marrickville. Almost half the population was born overseas and it is reflected in the various churches of the area ... Moslem, Greek Orthodox and others.

Burwood, due west of Marrickville, is one of the comfortable suburbs of the west, solidly residential and with a healthy shopping and business community. The National Trust has listed St Thomas Anglican Church (1848) and its neighbouring cemetery as part of the National Estate. Some magnificent old homes still stand in the suburb, a memory of when Burwood, like The Glebe, was one of Sydney's 'plum' areas. Shubra Hall, the former residence of Anthony Hordern is one of those

Downtown Parramatta may not look it today but the city is the second oldest settlement in Australia, founded on November 2, 1788 by Governor Phillip. Cottages such as Elizabeth Farm House (1793) surround today's town office blocks and shopping malls.

Above: Campbelltown, too, seems young and sprawling. But in 1795 the first settlers wound their way out from Parramatta. A town plan was first drawn up in 1828; now, more than 150 years later, Campbelltown is a city.

homes. Burwood, like Marrickville, has a large migrant population, but its actual population growth has been slight. In the past 50 years about 4000 additional residents have settled in the suburb. It leads a sleepy well-padded life, a cocoon in the heart of the bustling city.

South of Burwood, on that huge western and southerly push out of the city, lie the residential sprawls of Canterbury, Kogarah and farther south, Hurstville.

Canterbury is a middle-aged suburb, with a substantial number of houses being built in the booming 1920s. Land was first granted in the Canterbury district in 1793 to the Reverend Richard Johnson as a reward for being the first clergyman to serve in the State. He called his grant Canterbury Vale and held his first service under a giant tree. Sadly, the church he built in 1793 was burnt out five years later. Canterbury is a rambling area embracing suburbs such as Lakemba and Punchbowl,

Left: On the fringe of Blacktown a series of cul-de-sacs are surrounded by newly built houses. **Above:** Channel Seven's handy setting...in the tree-rich suburb of Epping. **Top:** Sydney's most exclusive footbridge... linking Park Road in Strathfield with Pomeroy Street in Homebush across the new Western Freeway built to take the pressure off Parramatta Road.
Over: Leichhardt...a mixture of inner city cramped terrace living, and suburban back yards. The shops around and in the suburb have created a little Italy, rich in pasta and pizza.

the heart of the Lebanese community in Sydney, and the suburbs which live on the Cooks River.

To the south lies Kogarah, at the heart of the St George district. Strictly speaking it is the south of Sydney rather than part of that general area known as the West. But the area is linked naturally to the west rather than the south by the Georges River which dissects the region. The active Kogarah Historical Society has done much to preserve the traditions of the area. Carss Cottage Museum has been opened at Carss Bush Park to retain the history of Kogarah. In Kogarah Bay and Oatley Bay the local council has reclaimed the foreshore to provide parkland. Up and down the St Georges River the speedboats and their jockeys live it up at the weekend. The opening up of the south began in 1843 with the road crossing the Cooks River at Tempe. It continued south to the St Georges River at Lugarno. The first ferry crossing was at Lugarno that year.

Lukes Bay at Hunters Hill...where Lyndhurst Crescent comes to an abrupt halt at a waterside home.

At Fairfield the commuters waiting impatiently for the eastbound peak hour trains to pull in in the morning, don't pay much heed to the station. But it is the oldest working railway depot in Australia, built in 1856 when Fairfield was the only link between Parramatta Junction and Liverpool. Fairfield today has a high ratio of heavy industry zones and matching high density residential zones. The Landsdowne Bridge over Prospect Creek built by convicts in 1833-36 has been listed by the National Trust. Fairfield and its neighbour, Liverpool, cover a vast area of the west, with a high population. But nearly 200 years ago the timber stands around Cabramatta were so heavy the area was called the Moonshine Run, not as a tribute to the illegal brew of the southern USA, but because timber on the run was so thick the moonshine couldn't penetrate. It's a distant picture today with kilometre after kilometre of high density housing. Again, migrants helped the area boom

Tiles upon tiles... the streets of Ryde blur and merge into one another in a sea of orange roofs.

after World War II with another postwar boom in the late 1970s when Vietnamese refugees settled in and around Fairfield, especially Cabramatta.

Liverpool has a special place in the minds of motorists who've made the long haul from Melbourne to Sydney. It's the nearly-home stage; the elation at having survived the Hume Highway and the sinking feeling that from here on in it's a steady battle with thick traffic. In the 1960s and 70s the population and migration explosion saw Liverpool develop as a major industrial drawcard. Now, however, the city relies on modern entertainment: the Warwick Farm Racecourse, the Liverpool Raceway which has car and motorbike races; a children's adventure land and the El Caballo Blanco Spanish horse show. But Liverpool does have a long and proud history. After Sydney, Parramatta and Hobart it is the fourth

oldest town in Australia. And St Luke's Church of England is the oldest existing Anglican church in the country, completed in 1824.

Fiercely proud *Parramatta* is the second oldest established town in Australia, founded on November 2, 1788 by Governor Phillip. The centre point of the West with its giant shopping centre and high-rise office blocks, Parramatta has been a city in its own right since 1938, at the same time retaining its rich history...Old Government House and Elizabeth Farm House are classic examples of early Australian colonial architecture. Elizabeth Farm House, built in 1793 by wool pioneer John MacArthur, is Australia's oldest existing building. MacArthur House, Roseneath and Hambledon Cottage are other majestic buildings preserved by Parramatta for Sydney. The Kings's School in Parramatta, founded in 1832, is one of Australia's leading private schools today.

St Ignatius College, or Riverview as its position justifies, dominates the horizon on Tambourine Bay Road. Behind the college Lane Cove stretches back, ultimately to the Pacific Highway. In front, the Lane Cove River separates Tambourine Bay and the college from Hunters Hill.

Paddy's Market, uprooted from its old home near Chinatown, but successfully transplanted to Flemington. Toys, clothes, trinkets and electrical goods: the market is packed with them. **Right**: Rookwood, Sydney's famous and sprawling cemetery. **Over**: On the fringe of Epping, two cul-de-sacs shelter a new cluster of homes.

Opposite: The famous red roofs of Sydney … neat boxes in neat squares. **Left:** The Mortlake Putney ferry weaves its way across the Parramatta River. The 15-car ferry has been in service since 1973, making the first run of the day at 4am and the last at 10pm. The 25.6m long ferry — DMR vessel No. 28 — was built at Carrington Shipway, Newcastle in 1960. **Above:** The two faces of the west — industry and housing — split by the Parramatta River.

Bankstown Aerodrome...Sydney's airport for small planes and also a centre for flying schools. Nearly 20 are based here, including the Royal Aero Club of New South Wales.
Right: The distinctive red roofs of Sydney. Flying by jet over Mortdale and Rockdale the red pattern is the tourist's first impression of the city.

Parramatta embraces Rydalmere, another pioneer settlement, Wentworthville, Rosehill, Granville and to the north, Epping.

Penrith, with its satellites of Emu Plains, St Marys River, Wallacia and Nepean River lies father west still, running to the foothills of the Blue Mountains. For most of last century it stayed a quiet agricultural backwater but it began to boom round World War I and today is a suburb in its own right. Although 50km west of the city Penrith is still in the commuter belt.

Windsor, farther out still at 56km north-west of the city, is rich in history. Today the cars whistle through Windsor on their way to Kurrajong, the Blue Mountains or Lithgow and Bathurst. But one of the delightful picnic spots of inland city is in the heart of Windsor, alongside the Hawkesbury and near Thompson Square. Windsor has the magnificent St Mathew's church designed by the convict architect Francis Greenway. The oldest timber building in the State, Rose Cottage (1817) lies nearby at Wilberforce and on the road between Windsor and Richmond is Fairfield, a Victorian mansion built for William Cox in 1833. Richmond, too, has its share of fine buildings ... among them another William Cox mansion, Hobartville, built in the Georgian style.

A journey through the spreading West can't touch down on all the points but it seems appropriate finally to look at ...

Campbelltown, a satellite city, a new suburb and yet one of Sydney's oldest suburbs. Campbelltown, with its intensive cut-price housing and housing settlements is one of the city's newest commuter zones. But it dates back to 1795 and some of Sydney's finest Georgian style homes were built in Campbelltown. Cattle which came over with the First Fleet strayed to Campbelltown. Governor Hunter found them in 1795 and named the area Cowpasture Plain. A town plan was drawn up in 1828 to service the 300 settlers who had moved to the area. Queen Street, Campbelltown, is the showpiece of the town's historic buildings with a number of buildings listed by the National Trust. The finest architectural offering is St Peter's Church of England, set off by the surrounding parkland. Campbelltown House at Minto, just north of the main centre, was built in 1812 and is another showpiece. Campbelltown, for all its newness and hasty suburban development, has a long and cherished history. Sydney without the West would be a duller place.

Left: Macquarie, the newest of Sydney's universities, has the advantage of being out in the suburbs with room to move.
Above: Darling Street, Balmain, comes to an end at the wharf, just an eight-minute ride from Circular Quay. Alongside the wharf the Peacock Point Reserve offers picnickers a view of the city. **Right:** Maritime Services Board tugs glisten at the jetty in Mort Bay just across from MSB depot at Goat Island.

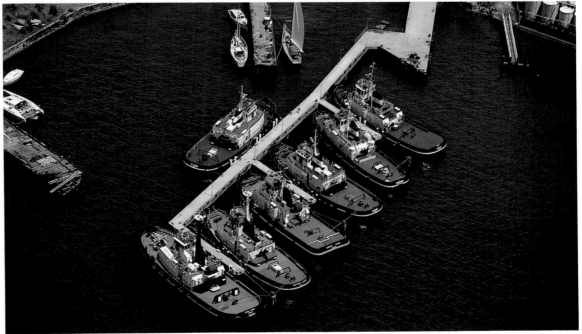

THE WILD SIDE

For all its vastness and its large population Sydney has a wild side. Places that are overlooked; picnic spots that are no longer fashionable; bays and inlets accessible only from the water. An hour's drive from Sydney is a walk through native 'jungle' harbouring large and unpleasant leeches. The developers haven't got to the whole city yet...

Kurnell, where it all began, is a forgotten junk yard these days. A

burnt-out Chrysler Regal rests on its side next to three garbage bags of bits and pieces. It's all a bit seedy. But there are pockets of Kurnell Peninsula, not far from Captain Cook's landing place where it's ideal for a picnic (though not on a windy day).

Even closer to the city, Balls Head Reserve on the lower North Shore is a forgotten picnic point, only a handful of cars go here, even on a brilliant summer weekend. And there's room to spread out. It is also an ancient Aboriginal site and carvings stand out on some of the ancient boulders.

Tens of thousands cram into Nielsen Park, Vaucluse, on fine days.

Left: The hire boats and private launches of Bobbin Head, launching pad for cruises of the Hawkesbury.
Over: Life on the lip of the Hawkesbury... an idyllic life on a lazy river.

But the cliff walks at the northern and southern ends of the park are relatively deserted. The views are spectacular ... straight up the Harbour and across to Bradleys Head.

In Paddington, the locals know about Trumper Park but few other people do. When the other city parks are crammed, Trumper Park is deserted. A handful of beagles and borzois bounce around with their podgy owners in pursuit, otherwise it's a small lake surrounded by trees and grass and abandoned. It's even accessible by train ... the Edgecliff Railway Station is barely 200 metres away.

The paths of Bradleys head are generally open and uncluttered ...

most weekend outings stop at the Zoo but the Head and its network of little mud paths brings you out on to a point with a spectacularly different aspect of the Harbour.

These are the city spots. Further out of town, but within an easy hour's drive are the genuinely wild spots. Rat Creek in the Brisbane Waters National Park is a hiker's delight, changing from dry scrub on the ridges to rainforest down in the troughs, with musty smelling ferns, palms and mangrove swamps.

In the southern half of the city, at Royal National Park are two of the most magnificent wilderness sites near Sydney ... Marley Head and Uloola Falls. Marley Head is on the coastal side of the Park, a primitive headland where the waves pound in. It is one of the most dangerous coastal strips around Sydney but surfboard riders swear by it ... enough to walk 3km from the nearest road with their boards for a day in the

The magnificent Victorian brick mansion Camelot, at Camden. The entire complex of gardener's lodge, stables and the home have been classified by the National Trust. Camelot was built for James White in 1888 and is a rare example of a magnificently maintained Victorian country estate.

tubes. There is a bush walk along the entire cliff edge of the Royal National Park but the direct and short route from the road to Marley delivers one of the best views and open picnic spaces in Sydney. Uloola Falls is on the inland side of the park. The bush ranges from wattle, which is friendly enough unless it gives you hay fever, to thick tree ferns which shelter leeches. A rocky stream runs through the area and you can almost guarantee a picnic by yourself.

But to enjoy the wild side of Sydney a boat is a must. Or a friend with a boat...

To wake up on a boat rocking on the gentlest swell moored under the

The rich soils of Camden provide a perfect base for the many stud farms in the area. Some are breeding properties; others are for agistment. **Right:** St Johns Church with its proud white spire stands out in the flat valley of Camden shopping centre.

Following Pages:
1. The Razorback, the hair-raising original route of the Old Hume Highway.
2. Narara...on the outskirts of Old Sydney Town, where a tent city springs up for the three-day Australia Day weekend rock festival.
3. Lake Burragorang...a natural reservoir penned in by the Warragamba Dam.
4. The marks of progress...power grids near Penrith.

Congwong Bay ... where the fairways and greens of the NSW Golf Course run to the edge of the sand dunes plunging down to the sea. **Below:** North of Hornsby, at the start of the tollway for traffic heading north, the pocket settlements of Cowan, Berowra and Berowra Heights gaze down from their hilltops on the creeks, inlets and bush.

western face of Pittwater is one of the true delights of Sydney. It's a long hike from the road at West Head down to the bays and tiny beaches along the west face. But a boat lets you go right into the secluded and sheltered inlets. At dawn the sun lights up the sandstone cliffs, picking out the knobs in cream and highlighting the dents with purple shadows. The banksias come to life with the daylight, a blaze of orange and red along the hills; a bad-tempered currawong who got out of the tree on the wrong side screams abuse at no-one.

Houseboats, powerboats, cabin cruisers ... they're all for hire in the Pittwater and the Hawkesbury. Farther up Pittwater, towards Scotland Island, are the magnificent shoreline 'suburbs' of Towler's Bay and Lovett's Bay. A handful of homes in each bay, sharing one another's jetties. The weekend ferry does the round of the bays and Scotland Island but unless you use the ferry or have a boat of your own they're inaccessible.

Along the Hawkesbury and up the inlets of the Ku-Ring-Gai Chase a boat is essential. It's possible to drive down to Coal and Candle Creek, or Cowan Creek but the bays of Jerusalem, Refuge, Looking Glass or Yeoman's remain a boating preserve. Brooklyn, the oyster town ... you can drive into it, but it's plain, a little rundown, an uninspiring village. From a fishing dinghy rocking gently 400 metres off the town it looks picturesque. You may not catch anything but it doesn't matter.

And in the south the same applies ... the Royal National Park forms the western wall of Port Hacking. A boat can reach the places where the roads are frozen out by parkland. Leg of Mutton Bay is a classic little bay where the native bush plunges down to the waterline as the Hacking River leaves the Park to join Port Hacking.

Even in Middle Harbour, where the suburbs fall over each other for a view of the water there are isolated spots where a boat can tie up for the night and the birds still make more noise than the far-off traffic. Off The Sugarloaf between Castlecrag and Castle Cove or tied in at Shore Beach off the Quarantine Station. There is still peace and quiet in Sydney.

Back where it all began ... over 200 years ago Captain Cook landed at Kurnell. Today Caltex produces oil at the site ... oil brought by giant tankers that would dwarf Cook's *Endeavour*. **Right:** The sprawling complex of Long Bay Gaol at Malabar.

THE WIND AND THE WILLOWS

GOVERNOR PHILLIP cut his feet clambering down sharp rocks, his nine companions were infested with ticks and cut by the thick native bush. This was 1789. Phillip was leading the group in search of farming land, starting out from the muddle of huts at the foot of North Sydney.

Today its wind in the willows country, the gentle gardens of the North

A house on a cliff presents its own problems ... where do you park the car and the boat? At this home in Battle Boulevarde, Seaforth, they solve the problem with a rooftop carpark/marina!

Shore with their English, out-of-place daintiness and the magnificence of the Peninsula where the wild westerlies and the boisterous southerlies sweep over the magnificent homes of the weekend retreaters and the long-distance commuters. The stockbroker belt of the North Shore and the weekenders of Palm Beach ... different types of homes but both beyond the reach of most Sydneysiders. And between them, Frenchs Forest where the hopeful executives make a temporary nesting place before moving west to the North Shore or east to the Peninsula.

When Phillip looked across from The Rocks he saw stony slabs broken by blooming wattles and banksias. Today he would see stony

towers lit by the blooms of multi-nationals, neon signs blinking Rand and Sharp and Sentry; fertile all year round. North Sydney was the original Sydney … the Aboriginals preferred it to the city land which they referred to scornfully as Warungarea … 'the other side'. The full cycle has run with many multi-nationals preferring to set up shop and house on the north side, shunning the city with its traffic flow problems and cramped parking.

The Pacific Highway dominates the North Shore, like a giant artery flowing off the Harbour Bridge. Little veins jut down either side as it winds through the greenness and out of Sydney.

The North Shore begins gauchely with the gargoyle of Luna Park staring out and ends with a mid-west American flavour, a caravan park screaming its five stars from the roadside. But in between is a way of life not found elsewhere in Sydney. Large blocks of land support large houses. Gardens flourish and English imports share the soil with native gums and eucalypts. This is manor house territory: hundreds of village squires happily ruling the roost together.

Lane Cove, Crows Nest and much of Kirribilli and Cremorne have become the flatlands of the North Shore. Town houses and blocks of flats squeeze on to the once rambling grounds of old homes. But above the TV towers of Gore Hill and Willoughby much of the North Shore has escaped the developers. Matronly old homes, with an apron of green in front, stand dignified, watching the cars pour up the Pacific Highway.

It's a far cry from those first maps of the North Shore with their cryptic labels … 'thick scrub, deep swamp' or in moments of desperation 'wilderness'. There were no Pymbles and St Ives then. No late Victorian and Edwardian homes standing among groves of trees with pedigree dogs dozing in the shade of an elm, too sun-drenched to chase the Siamese cat next door.

The upper North Shore quite prides itself on not being bothered by the beach crowd, by panel vans and pimples, old bombs and bikinis. But on the Peninsula the water is dominant. Where Church Point branches off to the left, the Peninsula begins. It's a different air of prestige; not as genteel, sometimes more ostentatious such as the suburbs of Newport and Avalon, occasionally even more reserved than the leafy North Shore … such as Palm Beach and Whale Beach. Here the rich have their weekenders … the media kings, the advertising whizkids and, above all, the graziers. The droughts, the floods, the plagues … graziers forever plead near bankruptcy. But an amazing number manage to keep their beach houses going in the face of such disaster! Once Palm Beach was the virtual domain of the grazier … a Christmas without descending on the Peninsula from the wheat fields and sheep properties just wasn't Christmas.

Left: A magnificent view of the Heads, Sydney Harbour's gateway to the ocean. The beaches of Manly, Harbord and Curl Curl begin the run up the Peninsula. A line of yachts trek from South Head on a long reach to Manly and the well-shielded Middle Harbour.

The southerlies rock the Peninsula, the westerlies can pound it for days. But the lifestyle remains untouched. The entrance to the Peninsula is virtually guarded by a castle ... Bungan Head where the ocean romps from Broken Bay to North Head on one side and Pittwater, laid-back and sunbaking, on the other.

A German migrant, Albert Albers, bought the tip of Bungan Head in 1919 to build his castle. From the castle along the sweep of Newport Beach and up the steep Bushranger's Hill ... the Peninsula winds its way to the end. Between Whale Beach and Avalon is the highest point on the Peninsula ... 115 metres above sea level. Here the northern

beaches coastline unfolds down to Manly and North Head. On the south side of this viewing point is one of Sydney's many oddly named spots ... the Hole In The Wall. It's a large cave which carries the name originally given to a huge natural arch nearby which came down in a fierce southerly gale. The cave, St Michael's Cave, is now taken to be the Hole In The Wall.

The Peninsula has its fair share of odd names ... Palm Beach, called after its palm trees, was much more romantically named Cranky Alice Beach. But perhaps it wouldn't have had the same appeal to the wealthy. Palm Beach marks the end of the Sydney's northern beaches ... the end

Blues Point Tower dominates the tip of McMahons Point Road. It was here Billy Blue, a Jamaican, ran the first ferry service from the Rocks to the North Shore.

of the houses but not the end of the view. Guarding the entrance to Broken Bay and Pittwater is the Barrenjoey Lighthouse. Below it is the old Customs House; smuggling was a popular industry in early Sydney. Rum runners found plenty of thirsty customers in the Hawkesbury and rum was often floated back into Pittwater. Long before Palm Beach became a millionaire's retreat the Chinese goldminers found it a restful place to smoke abalone ... and presumably opium ... at the salting works on the inland shore of Barrenjoey Peninsula. The Peninsula turns round into Pittwater, a backwater unaware of the ocean's roar on the other side.

Scotland Island holds pride of place in Pittwater, despite being a favourite spot for funnel web spiders. The little ferry that chugs around the island now drops off those who leave their cars at Church Point and get away from their work with a vengeance. At first they built lazy weekenders down on the water with a jetty for the yacht or cabin cruiser. Now the need is more desperate — the steep hills are being reclaimed and thick walls prop up the face of three and four-bedroom homes which stare at the calm water. It's a stiff walk from the ferry jetty to some of these homes at the end of a long working day but the view compensates for the effort.

From Church Point the road winds through the Ku-Ring-Gai Chase, past inlets and bays where houseboats and small cottage owners enjoy one of the most superbly relaxed lifestyles the city can offer. The road winds back to the Pacific Highway, easing the motorist back to the upper North Shore.

Pymble and Palm Beach offer million-dollar lifestyles; the pocket of the North Shore, centred on Mosman, lives it. Mosman and Vaucluse enjoy a rivalry for Sydney's No. 1 address. Vaucluse says it's more expensive; Mosman boasts more doctors. In this rarified atmosphere these seem to be the criteria that count. Certainly Mosman is the more

Above: Pymble Ladies College . . . a private school for more than 1800 girls from kindergarten level to HSC. The estate covers 25 hectares on the upper North Shore.
Right: St Ignatius College from above the Gladesville Bridge, showing the spectacular grounds.

gracious. The homes ramble more like Pymble. The beaches of Balmoral and Chinaman's Beach are more practical than the inner Harbour offerings of the Eastern suburbs. The richest pocket of land in Australia was once the preserve of one man ... whaling king Archibald Mosman. He applied for a four-acre grant (1.6 hectares) on Great Sirius Cove. With convict labour he built a giant jetty and a whaling station. In the 10-odd years he lived in the area he stretched that original grant to include a massive area from the cove to Military Road and from Cremorne in the south to Spit Junction in the north.

But regardless of claims and counterclaims no-one could deny ... even in the exclusive eastern suburbs ... that Mosman boasts three unique addresses. At Pearl Bay there are three houseboats with up-to-the-minute living, television, telephones, their own jetties and little roof gardens. The oldest, still carrying its HB 3 licence plate was built on an old barge. In the Depression of the 1930s, houseboat living was rife in Mosman. But it wasn't the luxury of today … necessity drove many people to live on the water, turning the area into a floating village slum.

While Mosman was begun as a whaling centre, it was developed in a hurry in the 1870s when the Russian invasion was 'imminent'. Panicking Sydney built Military Road to freight cannons to Middle Head and Bradleys Head. These, they believed, would protect Sydney from the hordes of Russians expected to flow south. The emplacements dug out more than 100 years ago are part of the National Trust Heritage today.

Specialised boutiques sell delicacies not far from where Mosman chopped up whale blubber and the gunnery crews stood guard. And between shops cupolas of every shape and description gaze down on the tourists heading to Bradleys Head and the Zoo. Domes and towers in copper, shingles, stones and stucco dot the Edwardian homes. There's witches hats and dragons, worn-out roosters and limp flags. The roads wind strangely around Mosman and Bradleys Head. Partly it is to avoid bumps and hillocks but more often a detour was made to avoid cutting across the corner of a gentleman's estate. Those courtesies are dead in Sydney today!

Sydney is remarkable for its number of natural and man-made boundaries. Crossing Middle Harbour, linking Mosman with Manly and the Peninsula is the Spit Bridge. The traffic pours down in three lanes, squeezes into two and then comes to a sharp halt … the bridge is up,

Like a scene from a European postcard the Cammeray suspension bridge sways over Munro Park, linking Miller Street from North Sydney to Northbridge. **Left:** The fortresses of Middle Head, built during the Russian scare of the Crimean War and today a peaceful picnic spot. **Right:** The Baha'i Temple in Mona Vale Road, Ingleside, dominates the countryside on the fringe of the Ku-Ring-Gai Chase National Park. The temple is open to all religions and all faiths and is nine-sided — nine representing the symbol for unity. It is one of only five temples in the world...the others are in the United States, Germany, Panama and South Africa. Two more are to be built in Samoa and India.

raised to let a lone sailor take his yacht through. The bridge may be man-made but it obeys one of nature's laws; something will go wrong when it's least wanted. If you're in no hurry the bridge is down and trafficable; but when you're running late, the flashing lights will go on and the bridge will rise just as you thought you were safe. For a moment that sailor avoiding the traffic jam and drifting out to the ocean is cursed. But it's too pretty to stay angry for long; there's time to loom at the houses clinging to the edge of the cliffs of Seaforth, anchored to the

ground by concrete pylons and accessible by rickety stairs or an old-fashioned inclinator. If there's a chance to build a house on the water, Sydney grabs it.

Right: Royal Prince Alfred Yacht Club at Newport . . . the base for Pittwater sailors and Hawkesbury drifters. **Below:** The ocean cuts itself and swirls on the rocks and shoals off Narrabeen Head where the swimming pool opposite North Narrabeen Beach offers safe bathing. Behind the pool the reserve offers a peaceful picnic spot.

Over: A Turramurra house that's almost a self-contained country club for a family . . . with its all-weather tennis court and a kidney-shaped pool.

Above: It's still Sydney's most 'exclusive' address . . . one of the three houseboats tethered at Pearl Bay. **Left:** Clifton Gardens runs down to Taylors Bay on the eastern side of Bradleys Head. Here, where Iluka Road and Morella Road meet, is a superb view over part of Sydney Harbour National Park out to the heads and back down to Rose Bay. **Right:** Obelisk Bay, a cove sheltered by Middle Head and unmarred by homes. The bay is part of the Sydney Harbour National Park.

Right: The natural richness of the upper North Shore . . . its trees. Every street and avenue is bordered by English greenery.
Above: The man-made richness — opulent living in St Ives and Turramurra demands a swimming pool and, ideally, a tennis court.
Over: Luna Park . . . reopened after the tragic fire of 1979. Its gigantic clown's face is now classified by the National Trust as worthy of preservation. On the water at Milsons Point, Luna Park is just a five-minute ride from Circular Quay in a small ferry.

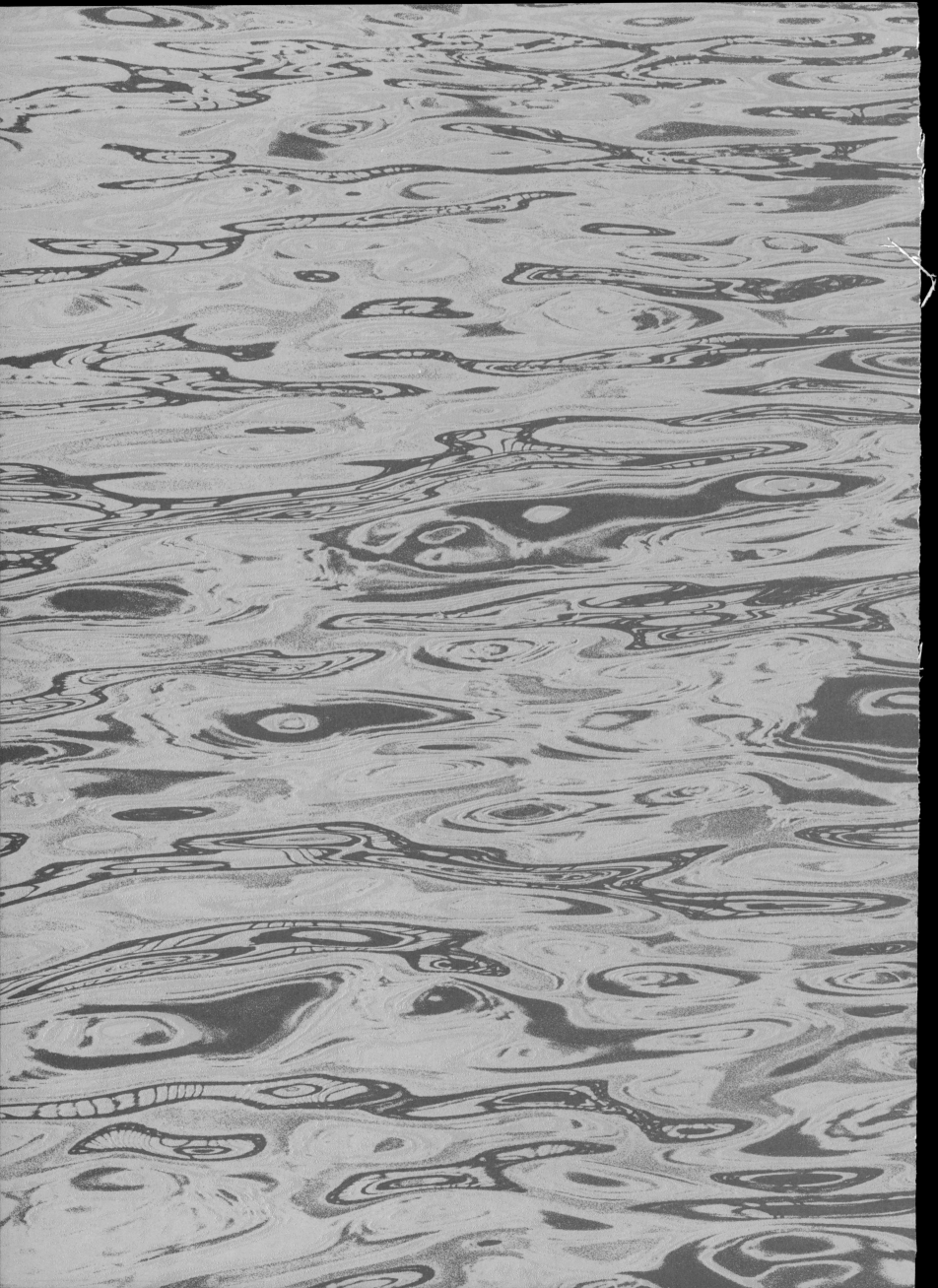